THE TRIPLE PLAY OF BUSINESS

A STRATEGY FOR A HEALTHY COMPANY

BOB STEINBERG

DORRANCE
PUBLISHING CO
EST. 1920
PITTSBURGH, PENNSYLVANIA 15238

Dorrance Publishing Co
585 Alpha Drive
Pittsburgh, PA 15238
Visit our website at *www.dorrancebookstore.com*

ISBN: 978-1-6470-2333-1
eISBN: 978-1-6470-2042-2

For my wife Janet,
whose patience and support are limitless

CONTENTS

"The way a team plays as a whole determines its success. You may have the greatest bunch of individual stars in the world, but if they don't play together, the club won't be worth a dime."

Babe Ruth

INTRODUCTION

EXECUTING THE IMPROBABLE

There are many aspects of a triple play that can be defined: The rarity of making three outs on a baseball field in a single play, the skill required by each player to achieve such a feat, the coordination and collaboration of all involved to execute this improbable event, and finally, the recognition that, to some extent, it is luck.

From the perspective of the batter, who is focused on driving in a run or at least getting a hit to advance the players along the bases, this would not be the outcome to be expected. In fact, of all outcomes, it is probably the least likely, even less so than hitting a grand slam.

And suppose, the fielding team, after a season of 162 games had barely made it into the baseball playoffs, and suppose that somehow they managed to knock off their playoff rivals to get into the World Series, and suppose that against all odds and all prognostications, they had won three of their last six games against their opponent in this ultimate seven game series.

Now it is the bottom of the 9th inning, and incredibly these underdogs are ahead four runs to three. Yet a one run lead is the slimmest of margins, especially since they have already allowed three men on base and there are no outs. One more hit could reverse their fortunes. Worse yet, the opponent's best hitter is currently batting, and with a 3 and 2 count, he is a walk away from scoring a run.

There is incredible tension in the field. And equal tension in the stands and the spectators are all aware that any hit into the outfield will drive in two runs, and all hopes for an upset will fizzle.

So, the pitcher now focuses 100% on the batter, and he knows that he must make that perfect pitch – a pitch that must have virtually no margin of error. His curve ball must just barely catch the bottom corner of the strike zone, forcing the batter to take a swipe at a marginal pitch and hopefully miss it completely, and thus strike out. But if not a strike out, at least the pitch must be good enough to cause the batter to pop up the ball for an easy out or hit it into the infield for a force out.

And yet, even if the pitcher succeeds in such an act of perfection (and somehow avoids pitching a ball and walking a runner in), he still faces two more batters. Yes, he knows the entire season rides on his concentration. Or better put, it rides upon his 16 years of experience, having thrown tens of thousands of pitches, having honed and improved his technique, combining great skill, hard work, and perhaps most of all, courage.

The pitcher ignores the crowd noise as well as the knowledge that millions of other fans are counting on him to execute the perfect pitch and at least get the first desperately needed out.

He is ready, and he somehow keeps his adrenalin in check. He contorts his body to get maximum leverage and winds up like a corkscrew…ready to release his curve ball with great extension and control…and then he snaps his wrist with just the right rotational force as he simultaneously uncorks his body to release this critical pitch.

The pitch is barely in the strike zone, and the batter struggling not to strike out, takes a swing that doesn't quite contact the ball forcefully. He has hit the ball into the infield, straight to the shortstop who quickly tags out the nearby 2nd base runner and then makes a perfect underhand toss to the 2nd baseman to force out the 1st base runner. But within microseconds, the 2nd baseman throws a bullet to home plate, whereas that runner is barely tagged out by the catcher. It is a triple play!

Pandemonium. The underdog has just miraculously ended the game and emerged victorious. Yes, miraculously, with the rarest of baseball events – a triple play, the underdog has just won the World Series, the ultimate prize, and no doubt their future will be secure.

I am not a professional baseball player, although I have had my share as a youth. But I am a business man. And oddly, this scenario I just described seems vaguely familiar. In some ways, it echoes what my business has been through, but one must ask, how so?

I started my business in late 2002 in a field I was familiar with. I had worked for three of my competitors but always felt that something important about their business was missing. Something that seemed under the surface just felt wrong. After three stints of four years, six years, and nine years respectively managing the sales departments of these three high tech manufacturing companies, I had come to learn that an important human element was lacking.

It was the lack of interconnectedness between employees. There was talk of common purpose, of being part of a team, of sharing the same goals, but it was merely a charade. It seemed to stem from how employees, customers, and vendors were treated by upper-management. There did not seem to be an authentic connection or respect for such individuals. Rather, there seemed to be a mere dependency on their existence rather than an honoring of their worth.

Compare this phenomenon to our heroes of the triple play. The triple play is the quintessential example of interconnectedness, of an authentic collaboration born of mutual respect and trust, where instincts kick in and decisions are being made in split seconds. Teammates are so connected and the non-verbal communication is so pure that the group outcome is one of perfection.

You see, executing a triple play can only be possible when "everyone is on the same page." And, unlike most businesses, where employees often feel diminished and begin to have their own agendas, the well managed baseball team has at its core a deep sense that every player is part of a greater whole. In other words, the level of respect that management has for players and the players have for each other provides the foundation of such a high level of collaboration that everyone's skills and hopes are linked to one another.

How does a company achieve that interconnectedness that breeds collaboration and fosters success?

It starts with an intention from the founders of a company that business is not just a profit hungry organization but rather a living organism. An entity that certainly must generate sales and profits to survive but one that achieves success and prosperity through an awareness that its employees are not just "hired hands" but rather the essence of the organization – the life force that drives the whole. Communicating such ideals may start with a company's mission statement, but all too often, the words are hollow. In contrast, by building a culture where every employee knows that they are respected and are further acknowledged for their individual contribution to the whole, that is the foundation of a healthy business.

By recognizing the humanity of each employee, they will begin to understand that they are the life force of the organization, and they will see that it is their individual efforts that directly contribute to the overall success and prosperity of the company.

CHAPTER 1

THE BEGINNING

Professional baseball teams have been competing for over 100 years. In that time span, needless to say, the system of recruiting young talented players, developing their skills through trainings and practices, and merging the new recruits with the more seasoned athletes is well established. And the business side of trading experienced players with another team or buying a competitor's superstar's contract is also well understood, albeit an expensive investment.

Not so, my business. I started my manufacturing firm with nothing but a concept. There was no building, no employees, no system in place, and certainly no history. Yes, I had nearly 20 years of experience running the sales department of three other firms, each of which produced a sophisticated type of gas flow meter. These meters helped industry to reduce energy costs, reduce pollutants, and increase efficiency. By accurately metering the flow rate or consumption of natural gas or compressed air, or a variety of other gases or mixes, companies gained the critical information to help achieve these objectives.

But I knew that starting a business had great risks, and like the triple play, there was a certain measure of luck as to whether the business would survive. However, if my company was not just to survive but to thrive, I needed a lot more than luck – I needed a guiding principal that would assure its success without compromising the ideals that I believed in.

Such a vision is easier said than done. Most companies start with a plan, and there is a focus on how to execute that plan, step-by-step-by step. However, my focus was to perpetuate a healthy company, and my definition of healthy is very different from that of any of the companies that I had worked for; and I suspect, it is different from most other companies as well.

My vision was for a company that honored and respected the employees we were to hire; a commitment to always be honest with our customers, sales representatives, vendors, and staff and a willingness to foster an environment of mutual collaboration. Beyond creating this culture of respect, I also had to differentiate our product from those that I had sold for during the past 19 years. That meant developing a much better flow meter as well.

So, like the triple play, collaboration, and trust in one another is a critical element, as is a culture of respect. And like the triple play, these elements are the foundation of a successful outcome, and in a deeper sense, they reflect the interconnectedness of each member embracing these values, whether they are employees of a company or players on a baseball team.

But first I had to find partners. I had the sales and marketing experience, and a colleague of mine (who also worked with me at two of the competitive companies) had the purchasing and vendor experience. So, we joined forces. Soon thereafter, we contacted another colleague, a very bright design engineer who we had worked with for over five years. All three of us were ready for change, and it was time to form a new business, a business that came to be known as Sage Metering. The three of us became partners in this new enterprise.

We hired our first technician, a quiet but very talented individual to build our products, that is once we were to have a product. So, we split up responsibilities, for there was much to do. The technician and purchasing agent went looking for a location to start our business, and I went looking for a source of financing. Meanwhile, the engineer was tasked with building a new type of gas flow meter. The competitors we had all worked for built a gas flow meter known as a thermal mass flow meter, a type of specialized electronic gas flow meter that reads the flow rate and consumption of gas due to heat transfer. Just as your body cools off from the movement of air, this product has a heated sensor that cools down from the movement of air and other gases. When it cools down, it pumps more electricity to heat it back up, while converting that electricity into a reading of flow rate or total. The product also needs another sensor (each made of a high grade of platinum winding) to maintain the accuracy, regardless of the gas temperature. We didn't just want to duplicate this technology. We wanted to dramatically improve it, and so we discussed the criteria we wanted to achieve to do so.

We discussed performance, we discussed packaging, we discussed features, we discussed customer benefits, we discussed how to differentiate ourselves, but most importantly, we knew we needed a major technical breakthrough. More about that later.

Meanwhile, as luck would have it, we found a perfect location to run our business and produce our product. It was located in a small industrial park, not far from the Monterey Airport, just ten miles from the California coast. The landlord was sensitive to our financial needs, and he agreed to lower the normal rent in the early years and we agreed to pay more in the later years. We signed the lease.

Businesses don't run on good ideas alone. We needed financing. What little I had to invest wasn't even going to last us through our first six months. It was necessary to secure a line of credit or some other source of funds. It was time to bring in some help in that arena; I contacted my accountant, a highly respected CPA, well known for his integrity, hard work, and good advice. With his help and the fact that his wife was on the board of directors of a local bank, we were able to secure an SBA (Small Business Administration) loan. Not an easy matter, however. A business plan needed to be written, and it needed to show how we were to grow the business to fund the interest and the eventual repayment. Then came the bank paperwork and an endless stream of forms and requests. But within three weeks, we incorporated the business, signed loan papers, secured a business license, and even had a well-known graphic designer design our company's logo.

As I began contacting sales representatives to discuss my vision for a new product, my engineering partner, who worked from home hours away in Southern California, began thinking about how to improve the existing flow meter technology. Meanwhile, the recently hired technician and my purchasing partner started outlining what our calibration facility would look like. No easy task since our industry doesn't just assemble electronic flow products, it needs to calibrate 100% of these flow meters. And to do so requires very sophisticated and very accurate calibration standards. Each of these standards needs to be traceable to a government laboratory called the NIST (National Institute of Standards and Technology).

So, each of us had our responsibilities, and we went about pursuing them with vigor. Since our engineer was off premises, we would have frequent correspondence with him, often with three of us on a conference call reporting our respective progress and brainstorming on how to best achieve our objectives. Then, off we went, working sometimes alone and sometimes together to move the process forward.

It was challenging but exciting. After all, we started with a blank slate: No reps, no facility, no production, no product. Slowly but surely, things started taking shape. We furnished our offices with the essentials: desks, phones, computers, etc. We began outfitting the production area with the necessary tools to assemble our product. The calibration facility was progressing as well. Tanks of bottled gas were delivered, pipes were installed, fittings were welded, blowers were ordered, and valves were deployed.

Meanwhile, we needed to source everything from platinum windings to custom circuit boards to special electronic enclosures, which meant hours of research by my partner with the purchasing experience. While he was investigating parts and components that he knew we needed, our engineer was designing an entirely new version of the thermal mass flow meter, which was yet to be defined, hence, most components could not yet be sourced, let alone purchased.

But the process continued and we immersed ourselves into the details, and slowly but surely, our company started taking shape. Many sales representatives who I had known in the past, who trusted my vision, left our competitors and signed up with Sage. Vendors, who my partner had worked with in the past, helped us by providing free samples for testing or at least reasonable pricing on these initial items. And updates from my engineering partner started showing great promise.

As we were approaching the month in which we hoped to have our first product, I began working with our graphics agent to build a website and to prepare to promote our company and our product. I also kept our new reps updated and gave them an early indication of the features we planned on including.

Within a few months, our progress was palpable. The calibration facility was taking shape and early tests were encouraging. Most importantly, we finally had an early prototype of our new flow meter, and already we knew that we had something special. Of course, it took many more weeks to complete the design effort and more weeks still to thoroughly test our new product and still more time to finalize the various configurations that we planned to sell. But as the culmination of all of this planning, hard work, and collaboration approached, our excitement grew. And although hard to define, we each began to feel a very special interconnectedness amongst ourselves; we could begin to stand back and see the fruits of our joint efforts in a new light. It started to become apparent that what we had been developing for the past six months was nothing less than a quintessential creative effort.

It wasn't long thereafter when we were ready to start selling and producing. But first, I immersed myself in all of the new features that we had developed. Unquestionably, we had leapfrogged our competition with salient differentiating features that the customers would welcome. The flow meter was novel. It had a large display that had a touch screen, so customers who wanted flexibility could make changes to the meter by simply tapping on the screen and selecting from a very versatile menu. For example, some customers wanted to use the meter in different pipes or change the maximum flow rate that it could measure. But most importantly, the meter had updated circuitry that combined the fast response time of analog circuits with the precision of digital circuitry. The result was a flow meter that was super sensitive and thus could measure extremely low flows (so low that even the gas running a pilot light could be measured). Yet the range of the meter was astounding. The same device could also measure flows that would be "screaming" through a pipe. This wide dynamic range is known as turndown, and we could measure flows over a 100 to 1 range and even resolve down to one thousandth of its maximum flow capability. But most importantly, our meter did not have the drift that our competitors had. Their devices tended to lose their accuracy over time, and thus, these manufacturers recommended that their flow meters be returned once a year for recalibration. That requirement had been a major liability for these companies since their customers were loath to pull meters out of a pipe each year and then pay through the nose to recalibrate them. However, our product was designed so that the digital circuitry did not drift, and thus, customers did not need to send it back at all.

In fact, we developed an extremely novel approach of reassuring customers of the continued operation and accuracy of the meter. The technique, called an In-Situ Calibration Verification, allowed our customers to go through a simple three-step routine to verify that the meter had not drifted, shifted, or changed since our NIST calibration when it was first sold. This procedure would take as little as three minutes and would even verify that the sensor was clean (if it didn't pass, the customer would simply remove the meter, wipe off the sensor, and reinstall it). A second check would normally pass, reassuring the customer that they could count on the accuracy of the meter and its continued high level of performance.

So, with a dramatically improved technology, a well-functioning calibration facility, and the beginning of a serious inventory of the necessary components to produce the product, we were off and running.

Chapter 2

The Early Stages

Dreams don't always manifest into reality. Our engineer began tweaking the design of the product, stating that the meter was not quite perfected. We didn't doubt his thought process, for we already had experienced how unique the current rendition of the product was. After all, we had experienced very positive test results. But we had a dilemma. I had been promising my reps a delivery date within six weeks, and it looked like the actual release of the product would be delayed an additional month or even two. I was not happy about starting off on the wrong foot with my reps. I had always built my reputation on credibility, and I had promised the reps (reps who had abandoned our competitor to sell our product) a specific and reasonable delivery date. Now I had to back-peddle.

I did my best to keep my sales force informed of our progress, but a few of them had orders in hand and the delays were beginning to frustrate their customers. I encouraged my engineering partner to do his best to speed up his progress, but he was not to be rushed. He was the type that worked best on his own timetable, as if his creativity would be stifled by outside influences. My euphoria that started a month earlier about our "interconnectedness" was beginning to slip. I wondered if that special feeling would ever return.

As I considered my options, I realized that I had to find the delicate balance between being overly demanding and risk setting his progress back, or being too passive and risk further losing the confidence of the reps. Thus, I seesawed between the two extremes while doing my best to pacify my sales force.

Well, somehow, we barely met the critical deadlines that some of our reps reported. A bit of pressure was taken off my shoulders. Soon more and more interest was developing for our unique flow meter, and our outlook brightened. Although it began slowly, the order rate started to increase and our confidence in the future grew week by week.

Progress is seldom linear. As our orders slowly started coming in, all of us felt very encouraged. We were beginning to sense that we were on the right track and that our fledgling business was destined to be a serious force in the marketplace. So, we began developing different adaptations of our initial product, offering customers more configurations, such as flow meters that had remote readouts or versions that were more industrial for those needing explosion proof enclosures. As we developed new products, we were also spending our capital at a more aggressive rate, assuring ourselves that the sales would follow to keep the profit picture in line. The sales did follow, but not as fast as we had hoped, and the line of credit we had, courtesy of the SBA loan, was beginning to diminish. It was time to get financial advice and there was none more capable than my CPA who helped us secure the SBA loan months prior.

His advice was "caution." He recommended that we seek additional financing by offering stock to others. We began by offering small shares to relatives, friends, and business associates. But very few were comfortable yet with helping us finance our company, even though we felt that their share in our growing business would generate more than a fair return on their investment. The few who did participate did help us move past some difficult financial times. But it still was not enough.

Ultimately, my CPA, seeing the potential of our business decided, himself, to invest. In return, he received a large percentage of our stock (e.g, a large ownership stake in Sage), and to protect his investment, he joined us as a fourth partner. Furthermore, he became a very important director of our young corporation, taking on the role of director of finance and eventually CFO. Of course, I, too, saw a very promising future for our business, and I decided to refinance my family's home to provide additional funding. Thus, our mutual funds seemed sufficient to move us into healthy profitability and positive cash flow.

CHAPTER 3

———•———

A GROWTH PERIOD

With sales coming in at a greater and greater rate, our meager staff was getting overwhelmed. It was time to bring in some additional help. Initially, we hired a second technician, a very competent and experienced individual who fortunately became available since the manufacturing company he had been working for during the past 15 years finally closed its doors. It was a stroke of good luck since good technicians are hard to find. In addition, he was a hard worker, dedicated, and had an excellent temperament. He was just the sort of person to fit into our collaborative culture. He worked in conjunction with our first employee, who now took on the role of production manager. The two were very compatible, and our vision of having employees who worked closely together was taking root. It wasn't long before we needed sales help, and in this case, we drew from a former colleague who we had worked with in the past. This came in very handy since this individual understood our technology, and he was comfortable working with reps and giving them guidance, including assisting them with their application. He also took on the role of order-entry, providing help with pricing, as well as model and part number selection.

I also interviewed an administrative assistant, an experienced woman who just moved into the area from Texas to live with her local boyfriend. She had tremendous experience in office management and was just what we needed to handle administrative duties. She was just the sort of individual we needed to keep the disparate elements of our operations running smoothly, and she could handle everything from office supplies to invoicing and was also a natural at answering the phones in a very professional manner.

It wasn't long before we brought in two more colleagues from the past: One to do the shipping and to help with assembly and one to handle quality control and to help set up some of our production systems. These two integrated nicely with the rest of us, and it was clear that we were becoming more like a family and less like a formal organization. Furthermore, all of our employees began reaching out to help one another. Each had a unique skill and set of experiences in the industry, making this cooperation invaluable.

Meanwhile, I needed to start training our network of national representatives to accelerate the rate of sales. To do so, I needed a working flow meter so I could demonstrate the unique features and customer benefits. We built up my own product demo, and I started scheduling training trips in different parts of the country. We supplied the meter in a convenient protective case along with a tiny battery-operated fan to simulate flow rate.

Off I went, spending a week at a time in a rep's geographic territory. I would first visit the rep's office and demonstrate the many unique features of our product. Then, armed with my working flow meter demo, I would join the salesperson at appointments that they had set up with existing customers (all reps also represented other non-competing product lines, and they already had relationships and prior business with them). In many cases, we called on new prospects, based on leads the rep had or leads that we had provided from the Sage Metering website.

I would power up the meter and show how sensitive it was by waving a sheet of paper near the sensor. Then I would use my portable fan to show the customer or prospect how quickly the display read the air flow and how the large easy-to-read digital display would show the ever-increasing flow rate as I brought the fan closer and closer to the sensor. The meter would also measure the gas consumption, known as totalized flow, on numbers beneath the flow rate. Of course, my demonstration was done with air, although many applications involve actual gas measurement, such as the flow rate and total of methane, natural gas, nitrogen, argon, carbon dioxide, or mixed gases. Essentially, I was simulating their actual application, which frequently involved gases other than air that were often part of their production process. In many cases, their concern was environmental, such as how much gas was being vented from their building. Or they may want to measure the natural gas or propane going to a furnace or a boiler to comply with local or statewide regulations or perhaps the flow rate measurement was needed to improve the combustion efficiency of the furnace or boiler.

An important application involved measuring the flow rate of compressed air, a common need at automobile manufacturers since compressed air is a critical requirement in such large industries, as well as in the food and beverage industry. Aside from determining by using our flow meter, whether they had efficient compressors or whether they needed more compressor capacity, there was another important reason to install a Sage flow meter: to determine if the piping had leaks. Since our flow meter had advanced digital technology, it had much more sensitivity than our competitors. That meant that if the pipes had leaks, our meter could detect even the slightest air escaping. Our meter was literally installed into the center of their compressed air pipes through a hole the customer had drilled and via a welded fitting that received our mounting hardware (e.g., we had mounting hardware that supported the ½" probe of our product – and at the end of the probe was the sensing elements). Since our sensor was in the middle of the pipe, it would monitor the flow rate if the compressed air was being used by operators throughout the plant. But when there were no operators using compressed air, the meter should read no flow. However, our meter is so sensitive that if the seals between pipe sections had started to dry out, then air would be escaping and our meter would detect even the slightest leak.

It turns out that compressed air is very expensive since it uses tremendous amounts of electricity. However, if there are leaks, it provides a path for the air to escape, especially since compressors run at very high pressure (about seven times the pressure of the air we breathe [105 psia vs 15 psia]). And typically, when there are even small leaks, one third of the electricity is wasted! That can increase a large company's utility costs by as much as $40,000 a year (over $3,000 a month).

Clearly, by installing one of our thermal mass flow meters for compressed air, customers can assess whether they have leaks, and if so, they can remedy the situation and save thousands of dollars a year, many times the cost of one of our flow meters. Essentially, our meter would provide a very large return on investment (ROI).

In my presentations, I didn't just focus on compressed air. Natural gas is very expensive as well. Thus, I would suggest installing our natural gas calibrated flow meters in the various production zones to sub-meter the plant's gas usage. This approach would help the plant engineers and energy managers to determine if certain locations were using more gas in their process than other similar locations. If so, it was likely due to an inefficient boiler or burner in that zone, and it may be required to optimize, or at least correct, the reason for the excessive gas usage. Furthermore, in large plants, upper management may need to know the total cost of producing a part or a product in a particular area. By sub-metering these areas, the overall gas usage in that zone is part of the overall cost, and that information can be fed to the accountants to aid in determining profitability of what they are producing in that section of the plant.

As I trained my reps or conducted my demonstrations, I also discussed how to bring the flow and total displayed on our meter's readout to the company's computers. All versions of the Sage flow meters we had developed had wiring terminals that would bring this information to the central location where the plant instrumentation is monitored. The meter had one set of outputs for the flow rate and a different set of outputs for the totalized flow. These terminals, where the wires would be connected, were well marked. Furthermore, the terminals where the meter would be powered were also well marked. And we offered a variety of power options: 115 Volts (similar to the outlets in your home), or 24 VDC, a common power supply at most industries. We also had 230 Volt meters for overseas applications.

Natural gas billing meters were at every plant, just as there is a billing meter at your home, somewhere outside your dwelling. In the plants, these meters can either be outside the plant or within the main building. However, these mechanical meters have limitations since they usually just measure the gas consumption, not the actual instantaneous flow rate. Furthermore, many of these instruments do not have outputs that go to the central monitoring of the plant. The problem with just measuring gas consumption (the total over a period of time) is that the meter cannot detect the flow rate, just the accumulated flow. Whereas the Sage natural gas flow meter is also measuring the flow rate, and thus it can pick up unusual excursions in natural gas demand. For example, suppose the shipping department has left the shipping bays open on a cold Midwestern winter day. By doing so, the natural gas is not just being used for the normal production of that company's product (such as the gas going to the dryers for the automobile paint process), but in addition, to keep the building zones warm. However, if the shipping bays are left open, a lot more gas is used for climate control than usual. The mechanical billing meter could not provide any information to alert plant operators of this waste, certainly not until the end of the month when the total gas usage would be reported higher than normal. In contrast, if the Sage flow meter were in series with the billing meter (in the same pipe as the billing meter), then its flow rate would spike and the company's computers would note the unexpected rise (via an alarm or simply a graphical or numerical representation) and an immediate assessment as to what is causing the excess could be investigated. As soon as a determination of the cause could be identified, corrective action could be taken (e.g., "close the shipping doors"). Thus, wasted energy can be quickly eliminated and the environmental insult could be lessened. Of course, many industrial users simply don't trust their billing meter, and they welcome an independent device mounted in a convenient indoor location, one that they could read at any time and see if there is a disparity between the consumption reported by the gas company and our meter.

My experience in having managed three of my competitors' sales departments gave me intimate knowledge of the workings of their thermal mass flow meters. As such, I knew the limitations of these products and could articulate the benefits of ours over theirs. Given our technological and ergonomic improvements, my reps were learning from me how to close orders for Sage, even when they were up against these much more well-known competitors.

Additionally, I knew the limitations of other technologies. In the event that I was up against a turbine meter or an orifice plate or a venturi or a pitot tube or a rotometer or a diaphragm meter, or even newer technologies like a vortex meter, I could describe their shortcomings. All of these technologies had limitations, the most common of which was that they need other ancillary instruments, such as a temperature transmitter and pressure transmitter, in order to accurately measure the mass flow. In contrast, a thermal mass flow meter directly measures the mass flow.

Mass flow, not volumetric flow, is what ultimately is read or recorded. For example, in environmental monitoring to meet local or national regulations, it is the mass of the pollutants that is being measured over time, not its volume, which determines its concentration and degree of risk to society. In the case of medical applications, it is the mass flow of the oxygen we breath (not its volume). In chemical reactions, it is the mass (e.g., lbs per hour), not the volume, that matters. And for a final example, the oil and gas industry delivers natural gas to their clients after the gas is separated from the oil extracted from the earth. It is the mass that determines what their client is actually paying for, not the volume.

Regarding all of these competing technologies, each of them requires that the customer also install a temperature and pressure transmitter to convert the output of their meter to the desired mass flow. A mathematical conversion is also needed to arrive at the mass flow. These extra transmitters cost money, and in addition, their installation adds to the cost (as well as to the uncertainty of the overall accuracy of the readings). Some of these meters have moving parts (such as bearings) that deteriorate over time and lessen the reliability of the readings. Others have a large pressure drop, which causes head loss, a term describing how extra energy is being wasted due to the restriction of these devices within a pipe.

Thermal mass flow meters, in contrast, measure mass flow directly (assuming they are calibrated with the actual gas), and they do not require the addition of a separate temperature transmitter or pressure transmitter to do its job. Without question I felt that I could draw business away from these other technologies, even if the companies who manufactured these meters were global behemoths.

Furthermore, with the improvements that Sage brought to our thermal technology (most importantly having eliminating the drift that required periodic recalibrations on an annual basis), we eliminated the main obstacle to the growth of the technology that had plagued the industry in the past.

With the strength of our radically improved technology and my understanding of the limitations of our thermal competitors, as well as the other technologies, our sales began to accelerate. As our reps gained knowledge of our product and how to properly present it and sell it, they gained confidence and contributed to the trajectory in growth that we were beginning to experience.

Clearly, we were on a path to success, and it was time to take additional steps to prepare for our growth.

CHAPTER 4

A NEW PHASE

It was time to hire an international sales manager. At one of my previous employers, I had hired an individual that I had known from another company many years prior. At that time, I hired him as an international sales manager to replace a woman who had just left. It turns out that he was currently out of a job but was working part-time as a consultant. I contacted him, and after a few interviews, he agreed to act as an independent consultant for us to set up our international distributors. He was bright and very experienced, and he was well-travelled. Over the months, he made numerous contacts, and he slowly but surely set up a network of distributors and soon we began getting orders from overseas.

Also, our CFO had a connection with a client of his from his accounting firm who did considerable business in Mexico. However, his market for his product was drying up, and thus, his Mexican sales rep needed additional revenue and he also had time on his hands. He set up a meeting for us with his long-term employee from Mexico. The meeting was held locally and we introduced this gentleman to our technology and showed him our operations. His English was excellent, but most notable was the fact that he felt he could sell our product, even though he had no experience with selling instrumentation similar to ours or even other types of devices. Of course, I had my doubts, but as I got to know him better over dinner, it became apparent that he was a very special individual. Aside from being very intelligent, he had a confidence in himself that is rare for most individuals, yet he was humble. He understood the opportunity that learning our product presented to him, and he felt he could do an excellent job promoting Sage metering flow meters throughout Mexico.

We hired him to be our Mexican distributor, and months later, I flew to his hometown to meet him, and we spent a full week making sales calls together at a variety of industries. It was helpful that I spoke some Spanish since I could then directly communicate with the prospects we visited. And if I didn't know a word, our distributor would teach it to me, or in some cases, he translated on my behalf. It was an encouraging trip, and within a few years, he started hiring engineers to assist him, and soon he became the top selling international distributor (in fact, he was outpacing some domestic reps as well). No doubt, Sage Metering was making good progress, and it was time to have a customer service department. One of our vendors was a sole proprietorship, and he had done calibrations at one of the companies I had worked for. Shortly after I left that company, he went off on his own to start his own operation and to do calibrations for other companies. From time to time, we needed his help to calibrate our meters when customers had very low flow rates. It occurred to me that he would be a perfect candidate to start a customer service department, in part because of his business experience but also because of his prior history as a technician. So I interviewed him, and after a bit of negotiation, we hired him. We had no issue with him working evenings or weekends doing calibration for others, but eventually this part-time work faded and we purchased his calibration equipment from him and brought it to our facility. Not only did he become our first service manager, but he also helped out the production department with calibrations. This was a perfect arrangement.

In addition to hiring a service manager, it was time to upgrade our inside sales process. The original salesman who was handling the order-entry eventually left. We were fortunate to replace him with a very bright individual, who had recently left a well-known software company. Although this individual had never been involved in any sales function, he did have an innate ability to provide technical service and support — ideal qualities to help reps and prospects with their application questions.

As time went on, he became one of our most important employees. He was the primary contact when sales calls came in, and he always could direct the caller to the proper flow meter for the application. He also could address virtually any technical issue. In addition, he developed his own techniques for order-entry, and thus was able to keep up with the ever-increasing sales rate. His efficiency kept the production department running smoothly. I must say, as I look back at my career, I have never worked with anyone who had such a high level of focus and dedication in virtually any task he took on.

Time doesn't stand still, and we needed an engineering manager in addition to my partner who had designed our evolutionary technology. Although my purchasing partner worked full-time on premises, my design partner worked in San Diego, a full eight hours from the company's location in Monterey, CA. As our good fortune would have it, an ex-colleague of mine from one of the competitors I had long ago worked for literally walked in the door. He was a brilliant mechanical engineer with a Master's degree, and he knew everything there was to know about the thermal mass flow meter technology. Although he had been director of engineering at the company we both had worked for, he had voluntarily left to work for a different type of organization. Unfortunately, that experience did not work out and he was looking for a job. But in this case, this was no hourly worker. I knew that hiring him would be a financial challenge since he was also being sought by our largest and oldest competitor.

After a lengthy interview, there was no question that hiring him would bring us to another level. But I expected quite a challenge from my CFO, knowing how cautious he was about spending money before we had the luxury of spending it. So I contacted my financial partner and suggested a luncheon with the three of us. Initially, there was resistance since theoretically this level of position was a bit premature. But as I described how talented this engineer was and how rare it is to have an opportunity to hire someone of this experience, he relented and a luncheon was set up.

At lunch, after introducing my ex-colleague to my financial partner, I simply listened and observed and didn't at all contribute to the conversation. I knew this gentleman well enough, that he was an excellent communicator. He is calm, collected, and has an impeccable character, just the sort of person that my partner would respond to. As I listened to the exchange, it was fascinating to see the softening of my partner as he was beginning to realize what a remarkable opportunity this was. By the end of the meal, I knew there was a good chance that my partner would be willing to hire him, even if it was well in excess of what we would otherwise fund at this stage in our growth.

Sure enough, we made an offer within two days since we certainly did not want our much larger competitor to get a chance to hire him. And so it was, our offer was accepted and he became our engineering manager. In spite of the tightening of our cash flow, this was the best decision that we could have ever made. We never regretted it, and our new engineer became one of our many shining stars, helping us to grow in ways we hardly even expected.

It turns out that the acceptance of our offer was in large part what our new engineer saw in us: A culture of respect, core values that aligned with his, and a company that values hard work and collaboration, as well as providing an opportunity for self-fulfillment.

CHAPTER 5

———

TRAVEL

As the company staff grew, it was important to keep the sales rolling in. I knew the best way to do this was to visit our reps and combine office trainings with numerous sales calls. They had the relationship with the customers, so they would set up appointments in advance of my visit. And I had the product to get their customers excited by identifying how our flow meter would fit into their operations. In the most general sense, our meter would either help reduce their operating costs, improve their efficiencies, or lower environmental insult.

For example, as mentioned earlier, customers may not realize that they are wasting energy by leaving the shipping bays open on a cold day in Wisconsin. Our meter would show a sudden increase in natural gas demand, alerting the operators of an issue. Or at waste water plants, air is used to oxygenate the aeration tanks to break down the sludge for further processing. It turns out that the blowers do not need to be running constantly to provide sufficient oxygen to destroy the bacteria. Rather our meter can provide feedback as to when to shut off the blowers, which can save thousands of dollars in electricity. In some industries, such as the auto industry, drying the paint on new cars is a critical process. The heat needs to be just right, and without our flow meter, it is very difficult to control the process. Even in steel fabrication, our meters are needed. The molten steel would form bubbles, unless the right amount of nitrogen and argon is injected into the vessel to stir the molten steel. Our flow meters provide the control to optimize the bottom stirring to eliminate flaws in the steel. And from an environmental perspective, furnaces and boilers simply exhaust excess pollutants, unless the mix of air and gas (e.g., the air/fuel ratio) is optimal. Our meter permits optimization of the flame, and thus not only reduces pollutants but also increases overall efficiency, which saves dollars.

It is interesting how many different types of industries can benefit from a high-quality thermal mass flow meter for gas flow and consumption. A few examples of the types of accounts the reps and I called on, and eventually sold to, include: food processing (they need nitrogen to fluff up the mayonnaise or gas flow measurement for their bread ovens); or for the glass industry (they use gas to heat the bottles, and air to convey the product); or the plastics industry (air is used to form the shapes of containers); or the beer industry (CO_2 is needed for the beer production); and the oil and gas industry (required to flare excess gas, and our flow meter can measure and totalize the output to meet environmental regulations); and in virtually all industrial applications, there is vent air that needs to be measured; and as noted earlier, compressed air to prevent leaks and compressor inefficiency; and natural gas measurement (in different zones for cost accounting, identifying process inefficiencies, or simply to confirm that the billing meter is still providing accurate readings). And, of course, there is a whole industry for heating, ventilating, and air conditioning (the HVAC market): where natural gas meters are installed for tenant billing in commercial applications; or at university and school campuses to monitor gas usage in gymnasiums and other buildings and/or to comply with local regulations for special energy credits (e.g., LEED credits).

Given the vast number of applications for our product, my mission was to educate my reps where the meters can be sold and how to present the salient differentiating features and benefits to their customers. As such I began traveling every other week. I went all over the country and often had as many as 15 to 20 sales calls in a week. It was exhausting but also exhilarating. In each case, I would listen to the customer as to what their business was about and what was important to them. As I developed an understanding of their needs, I was able to address it with the proper application and proper style of our flow meter. It was very rewarding to see the customer begin to comprehend how our product could solve a problem or benefit their company in some consequential way. As the customer was becoming informed, so was the rep. Furthermore, this type of "hands on" training would instill confidence in the rep, inspiring them long after I would leave to make successful sales calls on their own to promote Sage flow meters. So, the more trips I would make, the more the business would grow since I was imparting my product, marketing, and application knowledge to more and more sales individuals.

Yes, it was difficult to be away from my family, but I felt compelled to do whatever I could to help my company. Such a sacrifice is akin to what our champion ballplayers endure throughout their season. They, too, are on the road half the time. For me, I prioritized being away, knowing that it would directly benefit my hardworking employees and partners, their futures, and mine as well.

So, as time went on, our young company grew from the ever-increasing sales that our reps generated. In addition, our website, which had undergone many improvements, was also generating new opportunities. Furthermore, our international sales were gaining traction. We benefited from all these factors, and we began to feel that we were finally on a sustainable trajectory.

CHAPTER 6

———

AN UNEXPECTED SETBACK

Our sales rate had been climbing, and our hopes grew with it, but in the fifth year of our business, the economy slowed and we were not at all prepared for the implications. Just as we were beginning to feel that we had reached a threshold of stability, our profits began suffering, and so did our cash flow. With the associated overhead of all the new staff members, all necessary for our future growth, our company started feeling new pressures. We held out from taking any dramatic action for a few more months, but by the summer, we knew we had to act swiftly or else our financial picture would go from somewhat tolerable to a crisis.

This is when I called a company meeting and had every single employee meet me in the conference room. I needed to communicate the reality of the situation and to clearly state that we were all in it together. I could see that our hard working, committed employees were getting nervous, wondering whether the shoe was about to drop. However, I was focused on a somewhat less extreme approach to our situation, one that was more of a middle ground then what they may have had in mind. Layoffs did not make sense, if there was any way to avoid it. What was decided was a shared sacrifice.

I explained that I needed to cut everyone's wages back by 10%, including the owners, so that we could manage our cash flow until the economy recovered. But I also proffered hope, explaining that we had built up an excellent reputation in the marketplace and that we had a high-quality product that was well received by the reps and customers alike and that our high level of customer service distinguished us from our competitors. Surely, we would overcome this period of softness in the marketplace. We just needed to keep doing what we have been doing— work hard, work smart, and work together.

Again, the metaphor of the successful baseball team is relevant. After all, in a 162-game season, it is rare for any team to stay in first place. They have a long period of winning games and then they have a period of reversal, where the competition seems tougher, and they begin to go into a slump. But a well-managed team has cohesiveness and an ethic of meeting the challenge through continued hard work (practice) and a positive team spirit. Eventually, by supporting each other emotionally and having trust in each other, the downward trend reverses. Sure enough, they will regain that winning edge, and they start climbing right back up to the top of the leader board.

No doubt in their case, as well as in our case, a positive attitude is critical. It is not false optimism. Rather, it is an innate belief that the years of hard work are not in vain, and by continuing to work together our fortunes will reverse.

So, it came to pass, that a few months after my company meeting, our situation, indeed, did improve. In short order, our sales increased and the profits followed. We then made the decision to restore the wage rate to each employee, as well as to the owners, to what each had been earning prior to the 10% cutback. It certainly was a reassuring sign to our staff and I could tell that there was a palpable sense of relief, as I would meander through the different departments to see how everyone was doing.

The upward sales trajectory continued, and after a few months of sustained growth, management made an unexpected decision. We decided to restore the lost wages that the employees had endured during the cutback period. It was one of those decisions that did not come out of any long thought process. Rather, it came from a deep respect for our hard-working and loyal staff. They had accepted the sacrifice without complaint, and now we felt that we could reward them for their confidence in us. The day they learned of our decision, there was a quiet and deep sense of gratitude emanating from the employees all throughout the building. I could tell that this gesture on our part would have a permanent impact on everyone; for if they had any question regarding our respect and appreciation for their contribution to our group success, such doubts had evaporated.

CHAPTER 7

—•—

A NEW BUSINESS OPPORTUNITY

As the economy picked up, so did our profits. And we began developing new products and servicing new markets. A number of reps handling the commercial market known as HVAC (Heating, Ventilation, and Air Conditioning) began contacting me to see if they could sell our products. They were interested in promoting natural gas flow meters for sub-metering, such as for tenant billing or for sub-metering different buildings in a campus (such as a gymnasium or a cafeteria). The country was becoming more and more concerned about sustainability and conservation, and being able to monitor different zones of gas usage was becoming more and more popular.

At first, I had a bit of a challenge how to integrate these new reps into our existing rep network. The reason was due to our contractual obligations to our industrial and environmental rep network. The contracts of our existing reps offered them exclusivity in a given geography (e.g., New England, Texas, Northern

Jersey/ NYC, etc.). I certainly did not want to violate their contracts, yet these new reps presented an opportunity for a lot more business.

The solution was to negotiate with our existing reps in those territories where the new HVAC reps were interested in selling. In some cases, the older reps had no qualms with allowing the new reps to sell to that market since it did not represent a conflict with the markets the old reps were already servicing. Many of the older reps had no interest in the very price-driven HVAC market, and thus were willing to have an HVAC rep service the markets that they were not handling. In fact, there was a benefit: it was agreed that the HVAC rep would turn over business to the other rep if they inadvertently came upon an application from an industrial or environmental customer. In turn, the existing rep would agree to turn over HVAC customers who were interested only in climate control to the new rep. The only caveat was that if an HVAC application also involved a process (e.g., natural gas may be used for heating but was also used for drying of a manufactured product), then the older rep would retain this hybrid opportunity.

In a short time, we had signed up seven new HVAC reps. Once the first one had success selling our product, the word got out to the other reps to contact us as well. This led to a flurry of new business that we otherwise would not have had.

I learned what the common denominator was amongst these reps and why they were able to communicate with one another in recommending us. Although they covered very different parts of the country, they all represented the same Florida manufacturing and marketing firm, a company focused exclusively on commercial applications. This firm had a vast clientele, but their main HVAC clients were the dominant suppliers in the HVAC market: Siemens, Johnson Controls, and Honeywell, as well as their contractors. The latter will be familiar to you since it is probably the supplier of your home thermostat.

Given such a strong reputation, it occurred to me that I ought to contact their management to see if they could recommend some additional reps for other territories as well. After all, these reps were bringing in a great deal of business.

CHAPTER 8

A NEW RELATIONSHIP

I finally reached the vice president of this large Florida HVAC firm. My goal was to see if they could refer me to some of their stronger reps, so I could duplicate the success of our existing HVAC reps in other territories. We had a constructive conversation, but he said he would do a bit of research on the matter and get back to me.

After a number of weeks of not hearing from the VP of the firm, I tried to reach him but was unsuccessful. Over subsequent weeks, I left a few more messages and was curious and, in fact, a bit surprised that he hadn't returned my calls. But I persevered and we finally connected.

It turns out, that in lieu of sharing with me the contact information of his reps, he had an entirely different agenda: Rather, he wanted to Private Label our natural gas flow meters under their name and sell directly to their customers instead of having their reps come to us.

His interest in partnering with our company in such a manner took me by surprise. I needed a few minutes to process the implications. Essentially, this Florida firm had developed extremely close relationships with the three major HVAC conglomerates that I mentioned earlier (Siemens, Johnson Controls and Honeywell) and these "Big 3" HVAC companies were responsible for virtually all of the instrumentation for this market in the U.S.

In fact, the Florida firm also had products that they manufactured or purchased to specifically address the market served by these companies (e.g., chilled water flow meters, steam flow meters, BTU flow meters). However, what they did not have, but what they needed, was a natural gas flow meter, a product that we at Sage specialize in. In the past, they addressed this gap via their network of national representatives. If these reps needed to satisfy the requirements of the HVAC companies or their contractors or sub-contractors that were their customers, they would often purchase the gas meters from Sage. That demand for our meters is what led these reps to sign contracts with us.

It came to pass that these common HVAC reps shared their feedback about our products with the Florida company. They liked our quality, our customer service, and our delivery. And when commissions were due, we always paid them on time. It is no wonder that eventually the Florida company suggested we partner with them. The suggested arrangement was to provide our product directly to them rather than selling through our common reps.

To do so, they proposed the aforementioned Private Label relationship, where our natural gas flow meter would have their name and logo on it and the meter would have a blue, rather than green, electronics enclosure. Otherwise, the product was essentially identical to what we sold to our general markets.

But there was a catch. They wanted exclusivity for this market in exchange for selling a large quantity of our meters monthly. The concept appealed to us, but there would be an issue with our own reps.

Having earned the respect and trust of my national reps over the years, I did not want to restrict them from serving the HVAC industry, especially to those few reps who had already been servicing this market. This put me in a quandary since these reps could lose faith in us, especially if it looked like we were going after a big account at their expense. So, I negotiated with the Florida company, requesting exceptions for certain territories. They, however, had the leverage, and they were only willing to make a few exceptions. After thinking through the ramifications of restricting most of my reps from selling into this market but permitting the few strong ones to continue, I decided to go along with the Florida company's proposal. After all, my sense was that in the long-term, all of my reps would benefit from us being a stronger company. I felt that the benefit of having a significant and sustainable increase in our overall sales rate would offset the initial disappointment that my reps would feel for being somewhat restricted.

So, in January of 2010, roughly seven years after the founding of our business, we signed a contract with the Florida firm. The common HVAC reps no longer needed to represent us. From here on in, their natural gas flow meter needs could be filled directly from the Florida company. As for my own national reps, save but for the few who had the HVAC exception, I needed to inform them of our new policy. That is, they no longer could sell into the HVAC market unless the application was other than for climate control.

So, I wrote a carefully worded letter, introducing the new policy, acknowledging that there may be some short-term sacrifices but assuring them that there would be long-term benefit. I shared that this was a difficult decision but felt confident that we would become a stronger company overall. I predicted that this new relationship would allow us to have better resources over time, which in turn would provide us the capital to make improvements to our facilities and to our products that would benefit all of them.

Few people like change, especially when there is little warning. In the case of a group of loyal reps, it is important that they feel that their needs are being taken care of and that they can count on us. By restricting some of their sales, they may question our motives and perhaps feel anxious about their future with us. Therefore, I needed to underscore the long-term benefit, an assertion which to many seemed "hard to swallow." After all, from their perspective, how could restricting some of their sales be good for them?

So, I started receiving phone calls, essentially complaints from my reps for changing their contracts to eliminate their sales to HVAC customers. Essentially, these requirements would be referred to or filled by the Florida company. I explained that the only restriction was for purely climate control applications, not situations where natural gas was used for a process (for example, drying of paint in the auto industry) in addition to climate control.

Although the reps remained skeptical, I reminded them that their strength in their territory has always been servicing the industrial or environmental markets, not the HVAC markets, and that the possible loss of their business would be minor. I further explained that the Florida company would be generating a lot more business from accounts that our own reps never call on, and if we did not fill this need, our competition would. In a nutshell, our reps would lose little business. I then focused on the long-term where our overall business would get stronger, and this strength would lead to more products and features. Over time these new products would be available to our reps, which in turn would generate more sales. Furthermore, these sales would be backed up by greater resources to provide better calibration facilities and more support personnel.

Sure enough, the initial concern of our reps began dissipating. They adjusted to their minor restriction. Meanwhile, the Florida company's business for Sage grew. Within a few years, one fourth of our unit volume was from them, and eventually, their orders for our product represented one third of our unit volume. It was a win-win situation. The Florida company received our product at a very deep discount, allowing them to compete aggressively against other competitors, and we reaped the benefits of added revenue. Furthermore, even though they paid much less for our product than a traditional customer, the volume made up for the lower margins, and at the end of the month, they helped keep us profitable. This profit allowed us to begin to upgrade our facilities and to even consider hiring a national sales manager to further support and train our own reps.

We had a very strong relationship with this new partner, providing excellent quality, on-time delivery, and consistently good service and support. Also, once a year, I would fly down to visit with them, and in the evening, my wife and I would take their executives and their spouses out for a fine dinner, providing an opportunity to relax and to get to know one another better. It was comforting to have such a positive relationship with a Private Label partner that was flourishing.

It wasn't long before their parent company was making overtures to us as to whether we would be interested in being acquired. This was a slow process since initially we had very little interest in losing our independence. Furthermore, we were very concerned about their ultimate intentions. We certainly did not want to sell if it meant them closing our facility or having them slash our loyal employees from the payroll. We were skeptical, and as such, we were showing little enthusiasm for being purchased and the discussions became less frequent. Nevertheless, periodically they would check in with us to see if our position has changed. Of course, we were doing fine without them, and we continued focusing on and improving our markets and building our sales and reputation.

Meanwhile, we would have annual sales meetings at Sage, where we would invite our reps to Monterey and review the product features, discuss market opportunities, address selling techniques, conduct a plant tour, and have an awards dinner in the evening where spouses were welcome. These events were great fun, and it really helped our reps to bond with us. Sure enough sales would pick up after these sales meetings, not only from the attendees but from the other staff in their offices as well. The new material that we developed for them would get distributed to others and they, too, would get motivated to more aggressively push our products.

CHAPTER 9

———

A NEW GROWTH PERIOD

Business started humming. Our reps have adjusted to the restriction of not being able to sell into the commercial market, and as expected, they did fine selling the Sage products to their core industrial and environmental markets. The economy was gaining strength and our reps were getting stronger, both in terms of their understanding of how to convey our unique features, as well as in their confidence in selling our products. Meanwhile, each month, the Florida company was purchasing ever greater numbers of Private Labeled flow meters from us. This led to a significant boost to our profitability in spite of the heavy discounts they were entitled to by contract. It was a good period for all of us.

It allowed us to give raises to our well deserving employees and to make improvements to our facilities. It also took some of the pressure off my shoulders, as well as that of my CFO, since in the earlier years, cash flow was always a challenge.

This period of prosperity in 2010, 2011, and 2012 led us to justify some additional hiring. I was getting a bit burned out from making sales trips, even though at a less frequent rate than the early years. It was time to hire the national sales manager that recently we were considering. I went through my resume file and found one candidate that seemed to be qualified. In fact, he was originally referred by an existing and well-respected rep, but at that time, we could not justify hiring him. I doubted he was still available but chose to give him a call anyway.

Surprisingly, he answered his phone since he had just recently left a job that did not work out. After a number of Skype and phone interviews, we decided to hire him. He seemed like a perfect candidate, especially since he had a very strong marketing background in addition to his strength in having sold industrial and process control instrumentation. He was middle-aged, very experienced, and a hard worker. Furthermore, he lived in Chicago and this made it possible for him to easily fly from O'Hare to any other part of the country or even to drive directly to Mid-Western appointments.

So, after a week of factory training in Monterey, he started scheduling rep visits to make sales calls and to reinforce rep selling techniques. He also began identifying areas in the country where the reps were not motivated. Although he would do his best to reinvigorate them through his sales trips and phone support, in some cases, the reps still were not motivated. These areas were ripe for switching to a new rep organization. In other cases, there were a few territories that were not yet being serviced, which also needed representation. So, in addition to training our existing reps, his experience with rep networks in the past opened up the door to interview more appropriate organizations, assuming they were not selling (or not happy with) competitive products.

As it turned out, he added a few strong rep organizations that were willing to take on the Sage flow meters in addition to their existing non-competing product lines. These reps eventually got trained (in some cases, I joined the national sales manager for the introductory training), and in short order, they began selling our products. Furthermore, the newer reps were more aligned with our new effort, which moved us into a more industrial focus. That is, in our early years, our products were general purpose for light industry or environmental applications. But as we have grown, our products have come to be designed for more heavy-duty industries (e.g., steel, aluminum, and oil and gas industries). As our reputation grew, so did our customer base. We were beginning to attract higher quality rep organizations to help us in our marketing and selling efforts.

Understandably, a new national sales manager plants a lot of seeds, long before his efforts turn into actual sales. The key is to build activity, to train and support the reps, and to keep in close touch with them to gain mindshare (i.e., to get them to devote more of their valuable time to Sage - not just to their other products). The implication, of course, is that when new employees or new reps are hired, the future will always look brighter than the present. In a sense, there is this period of development that, if handled properly, will inevitably translate into profits.

During this transitional time, the company (e.g., Sage) is essentially funding the effort. We had no problem doing so, as long as we had confidence that we were on the right track and that the efforts by the sales manager would eventually pay off.

And we did have confidence. So, when the opportunity arose to hire one of our competitors' disenchanted employees to run the service department, we did so. This gentleman had worked with me at one of the other companies I had worked at, and he had solid credentials. It also gave us the opportunity to move our previous service manager into a position of test engineer, so that we could more thoroughly evaluate the performance of different phases of our product development. Also, he had sales experience, especially in South America, and this helped offload our international sales manager.

Naturally, hiring new staff in 2013 added to our overhead, but we still managed to end the year with a decent profit. We felt confident that these additional professionals would move us to a new level in sales and support over the next year or so and that the profits would continue.

CHAPTER 10

A SERIOUS PERSONNEL CHALLENGE

So, it seemed that we had the staff we needed to grow our company to the next level. With the addition of the newly hired engineering manager, as well as the recently hired international manager, we felt that these new positions would provide the foundation for solid growth. And having also added a new service manager, we were prepared to deal with any customer issue that could develop.

But as time went on, our design engineer, the partner who developed our product, seemed to have a bit of an attitude. Even though he became our vice president of engineering at the time we hired our new engineering manager, the two did not appear to get along. Since our engineering manager is naturally personable and has always gotten along with everyone, regardless of position or job description, this situation seemed to be very unusual. My personal intervention to bring the two together was unsuccessful. I always took pride in my ability to be the diplomat, to find common ground, but in this case my efforts to bring reconciliation fell hollow.

It certainly put me in a challenging situation: As the president of the company, by all rights, I could have forced the issue (i.e., demanded a change in attitude by my partner, or else). But my better instincts held me back. For one thing, it is anathema to our culture of collaboration and mutual respect to act in such an authoritarian manner. Furthermore, as much as I tried to reconcile the situation, the vice president had a strong defensive streak. He took everything personally. It didn't matter whether it was a constructive suggestion about his design, which he took as criticism, or a suggestion to show respect in his communications with staff members, which he denied was necessary. In fact, he never would take responsibility for his manner of speaking with others but rather would blame the breakdown in communication to the other's lack of understanding or lack of respect for him. It was as if he was always in the right, and the staff member just didn't get what he was conveying.

Over time it was not just the engineering manager who had problems with the vice president. Other staff members would voice some concerns about a product feature not quite working right, and he would always blame the issue on the technician not performing something properly or the customer not understanding how to apply the product. He never took the input as valid, and thus he never took any responsibility. I came to learn that his behavior was based on his belief that no one was as smart as he was. He either disregarded input from others, or worse yet, would patronize those he did communicate with.

I, too, had issues. He had a way of twisting my words around. He would always come up with a defense, which in some cases was a barrage of obfuscation, and in other cases, outright dismissal of my input. His twisted logic and attitude, bordering on insubordination, was unacceptable. Furthermore, his management style was counterproductive. Our hard-working engineering manager reported to him, and any contrary idea or approach that he presented to his boss was rejected.

Clearly, this was not healthy for our employees and certainly undermined the cooperative spirit that was the foundation of our culture. And it got worse. The more all of us tried to temper his "holier than thou" attitude, the more he resisted. His behavior became outright toxic.

It was time to take some strong action. Yet I knew that we needed him "to be on board." His designs and product development were essential to our success and growth. Furthermore, he spent months writing the software code that runs our flow meters, and he refused to turn over a copy of this confidential source code to our main office for safekeeping. He would give us numerous excuses why he could not deliver it to us (i.e., it is too proprietary to duplicate since it may get into the wrong hands; or it was encrypted in such a way that we could not use it anyway, or he would claim that no one had the understanding at the factory of what to do with it, so why risk sending it to us). Although, by all rights, it was the property of Sage, not his. He seemed to have this belief that it was his "baby," and he should be the keeper of the goods. Eventually, I persuaded him to turn over what he had, but I never was able to open up the files that he furnished, regardless of being given an encryption passcode. He claimed I had everything I needed to open it up, yet I could not convince him that there was a flaw in what he had provided. So I left that battle for another time.

Although the software code issue could be resolved at a future time, the toxicity of his behavior towards others could not be ignored. In particular, his attitude towards our engineering manager was worsening, and I was now worried that I may lose this important individual to frustration. After all, he was caught in the middle: His boss was berating him, yet he worried that going around him by confronting me with his concerns might backfire.

I had no choice but to take strong action. But I did not want to discourage my partner from continued progress on our product by stripping him of his authority as an original partner and director of the company. But I did need to find a middle ground.

So, off I went to San Diego, setting up a meeting which I described as critical without defining the details until I actually arrived. I recommended we meet at a local restaurant rather than at his office, wanting to be in a neutral environment. He arrived on time, and I told him we would get to the point of my visit soon enough, but first, let's simply have a bite to eat and get caught up. After having had a delicious and relaxing meal, I "cut to the chase." I said we have some serious morale issues and I need to make some changes. I explained as best as I could that his attitude was a severe problem and that it was contaminating the others at Sage. We could not have that. I recognized his brilliance as an engineer, but I also described the implications of this natural tendency of his to criticize others and to unwittingly demean them. Of course, he tried to defend himself, but I "kept on message" and stood firm on the facts as I saw them. He simply was causing more damage being a manager of others than he even realized. It was time that the roles needed to be reversed. I then removed him as vice president of engineering and defined his new role as chief technology officer (CTO). It was not a demotion, rather recognition that he was better suited focusing on product development and being a resource for any of us needing technical assistance. Essentially, by removing his management responsibilities, he would have more time to focus on his strengths and his natural creativity. He understood the new role but did not like the implications of what I said next.

"Now that you are excused from being the vice president of engineering, the engineering manager will become the director of engineering. He will manage the department, and he no longer reports to you."

That was a shock to him. After all, he had been criticizing him for months, implying that he was not technically up to par, and now I am appointing him as director and the overall manager. My own observations and that of my other two partners were totally inconsistent with this partner's assessment. We all felt that the engineering manager had been doing an extraordinary job and clearly his demeanor was exemplary and his management skills were very strong. As such, I knew that this new appointment to director of engineering, reporting to me rather than to the now CTO, would be necessary and a big boost to everyone's morale. I thus underscored my reasoning and appealed to our new CTO to learn to be a team player rather than a loner. I further encouraged him to feel free to make bi-monthly visits to our main facility, where he could suggest any operational or technical improvements to our calibration or production systems. After all, I noted, "You have a special talent for discerning areas that need improvements, given your technical experience and your natural ability to process and view your surroundings on multiple levels."

My mission was accomplished. When I returned to Sage headquarters, I officially appointed my engineering manager to that of director, and he was thrilled. Knowing that he could now proceed unimpeded and he would report to me directly, he was like a new man. As far as I could tell, we had dodged a bullet. Somehow, I got through to our obstinate partner and felt that he was capable of absorbing the emotional blow and would continue to work hard to help us grow. At last, all hands were on deck!

CHAPTER 11

A MID-YEAR CRISIS

Sales were coming in nicely, and for the time being, I could focus on growing the business rather than dealing with the distraction of personnel issues. As the months went on, I put my energies into supporting my staff and helping where I could. I kept my pulse on the efforts of my national sales manager and continued to monitor whether our operations were running smoothly. In addition, I made a few trips to oversee our booth at two different trade shows, as well as a few trips to assist in training new reps.

Unfortunately, at one of our weekly meetings, there were reports that the Florida HVAC company, who now represented one fourth of our overall sales volume, had complaints from one of their customers that the accuracy of our flow meters was off. This caught us by surprise since for years we have been diligent in maintaining our high accuracy calibration standards, and we had been consistent in sending them out for their expensive semi-annual recertifications. Furthermore, our production department frequently checked all pipe fittings for leaks and engineering would periodically verify that everything was working properly in our calibration system.

There was no obvious indication of any issues in our calibration facility, so we asked the Florida company to furnish us more details so we could get a handle on what portion of the calibration appeared to be off.

Normally, we have direct contact with a customer when there is a service issue, but in this case we were not given permission to speak directly with their customer. It made us a little suspicious whether the problem wasn't due to the end-user's method of testing or perhaps as to how they had installed the meters. But we certainly did not want to criticize their customer without exhausting all other possibilities.

Eventually, a third party (an independent testing agency) was given the questionable meters and there did seem to be a problem. However, we were not able to find the source of the issue on our end. We spent days trying to diagnose what could be causing the inaccuracy and still could not identify any particular cause. This was not only frustrating to us, but it was particularly frustrating to our Florida partner since they claimed that this issue was jeopardizing a large potential of business.

We continued to investigate and, of course, put our primary focus, effort, and attention on resolving this issue. We ended up checking every single element of our calibration system in a sequential manner. Although we did not yet find a smoking gun as the cause, there did seem to be some inconsistency between one of the turbine flow meter standards that was recently recertified. We went so far as to challenge the turbine vendor and asked them to verify their work. So, we sent that standard back to them for retesting and temporarily used a spare turbine and its fitting. The spare seemed fine since the larger turbine flow meter, at its low range, overlapped the smaller turbine meter at his high range, and they both agreed.

The turbine vendor declared that there was no error in the turbine. This seemed hard to believe since it was the last possible source of error. When the retested turbine flow meter standard was returned, we installed it and it seemed to work fine, as checked against our larger turbine meter. But in an abundance of caution, we switched back to the small connecting fitting that was removed from that meter before it was shipped to the vendor. We replaced the current fitting with the previous fitting. Both fittings seemed identical since they both had the same outer diameter and length. However, shockingly, the readings with this fitting did not agree with the ostensibly similar other fitting.

We were aghast. What could be different? Well, it turned out that this small connecting fitting (which sometimes we changed out during recertifications and sometimes we didn't) apparently had an inner diameter that was slightly different from that of the inner diameter of the other fitting. This was highly unusual since most pipe fittings are standard, both in terms of outer and inner diameters (i.e., they have the same wall thickness). Apparently, this was an anomaly, and to say the least, a very unusual situation.

Worse yet, our meters depend on consistency in inner pipe dimensions. Any percentage variation in the expected diameter results in a much higher variation in terms of its cross-sectional area due to the error being squared (e.g., let's say that the diameter is 2% smaller, then the error would be 2% x 2% or 4% worse!).

Wow, what a surprise. The error that the end-user was seeing was directly a result of which fitting we happened to have installed. In some cases, when we recertified the turbine, we changed the turbine and the fitting, and in other cases we just changed the turbine itself. So, there was no way to know how many meters had an associated calibration error (since we had no reason prior to this discovery to need to document whether the fitting was or was not changed).

What a dilemma this was. Since our Florida HVAC customer not only had this large potential client who had the complaint, but they also had close to 100 of our previously calibrated meters in their stock. So, the question was: How many of the meters in stock also had the same error? This was an unknown.

The consequences of this uncertainty were very serious. Our Florida customer could not tolerate having meters that did not meet the published accuracy specifications and as noted, it could not be determined how many of their Sage inventory actually had the error. Thus, they insisted that our service department recalibrate all of these nearly 100 meters all over again (of course, using the correct fitting). This was a large and expensive undertaking and one that would strain our time and financial resources to the limit. But there was no choice. We needed to bite the bullet and accommodate their request. The only saving grace was that all of their natural gas flow meters had a relatively low flow rate, and the cost of the methane we used to calibrate them was tolerable.

It took us four weeks, but we managed to work it in with our normal calibrations on new meters. Shortly after this month-long effort was completed, their upper management, their service manager, and the main flow engineer of the Florida company planned a visit to our facility to observe our calibration methods and discuss our preventative maintenance strategies to avoid any recurrence of issues in the future.

When the delegation finally did arrive, we were well prepared. We went through every step of our quality control and calibration procedures, starting with incoming inspection of parts to the systems used to generate a work order, to the assembly of the meter, to the pre-calibration operation known as temperature calibration, and finally to the gas flow calibration of the meter. Regarding the latter, we went through the dozens of steps taken to calibrate a meter. Every phase was demonstrated, including how we hook up the methane tanks, how we purge the lines from previous calibrations, how we choose the proper pipe size for calibration, how we install the meter, and how the actual calibration is achieved. It was highly informative for them as I could see that they were taking very good notes during the overall process. If they had any questions about any phase of the operation, we would respond and go into more detail or at least clarify what they were observing.

That night we went to dinner at a well-known seafood restaurant. The food was great, but the camaraderie was even better. We were having such a good time that on at least three occasions, the waiter asked us to quiet down since we were disturbing nearby diners. We finally obliged.

The next morning, our guests stayed back at the hotel to have their own private meeting to discuss and document their observations and to list any suggestions they had to share with us later that day.

Shortly after lunch they returned to Sage, where we met in our large conference room to hear their feedback. They thanked us for our positive response to the crisis and applauded our willingness to accommodate their request to recalibrate the dozens and dozens of meters that they would send us from their inventory. They further acknowledged our diligence and commitment in producing a quality and high performing product and they also appreciated our systematic approach in having uncovered the root cause of the calibration issue.

However, they had many more years of experience in running a business than we had, and clearly their operation was much more refined than ours was. As such, they had numerous suggestions to further improve our systems and our testing methods in order to prevent problems. The following list covers most of their observations and comments:

- Eliminating gas leaks should be a very high priority. If you improve this part of the system, you will reduce calibration errors and increase throughput.
- Tie the gas analyzer into the automation system to test and record the gas mixture before and after every run. This should detect leaks to the atmosphere as they occur.
- Establish system checks designed to detect leakage in parallel test pipes. These checks need to be very sensitive and capable of detecting small leaks.
- Improve the method for inserting and removing meters from a charged piping system, so gas loss will be minimized. Perhaps this can be accomplished with the use of isolation valves.
- Install alternate technology secondary reference meters to continuously validate turbine meter, pressure, and

temperature sensor performance. We can work with you to provide low cost vortex meters if you want to use them.

- Fully validate the automation system as quickly as possible.
- Create written process instructions for the temperature and flow calibration. Train operators on using the written procedures.

We appreciated their input, and by the end of the day they headed back to their hotel with plans to return to Florida early in the morning.

(Over time we did implement virtually all of their suggestions. Of course, the automation was the biggest challenge, but two years after their visit we had completed the difficult challenge and highly technical deployment of automating our calibration facility).

Needless to say, we were relieved that, once again, all was well with this most important customer and we knew that our relationship, as strong as it had been, had become even stronger.

This experience was a big test for us, but we prevailed. In thinking about how the other companies I had worked for would have handled this challenge, I doubt they would have stepped up to the plate. Most companies, including the three competitors I had worked for, tended to be so focused on the bottom line that they would rarely go the extra mile in supporting a customer, as the demands to do so would have become costlier and costlier. Our decision to take the extraordinary step of recalibrating 100% of the inventoried meters that they had purchased was very difficult in terms of manpower, disruption to our normal operations, and of course, to our profitability and cash flow. Rather than negotiate with them to share the costs or perhaps to take a middle road of putting a correction factor in their meters, we went all out. Our commitment "to put the customer first" shows character and caring. Clearly, our culture of mutual respect goes well beyond our own employees. Applying the resources needed to solve the problem in a timely fashion was challenging; after all, we were already putting our full energies into growing the business even before this situation developed. But together, through collaboration, extra effort, and a perspective that our customers are our most important asset, we dealt with the crisis. And yes, we could have failed to meet the challenge, but like our World Series victors, we, too, became victorious.

CHAPTER 12

———

IS OUR DESTINY BEING DENIED?

A few weeks after all was well with our Florida company and all appeared back to normal, I went on a one-week vacation on the East Coast to join 16 of my family members and close relatives to celebrate my mom's milestone birthday. I had found a beautiful six room rental in a gated community on Kiawah Island in South Carolina. The weather was perfect, and all of us were enjoying the pool, the nearby white sand beach, biking, hiking, and simply enjoying each other's company.

However, in the middle of the vacation, I received an urgent call from my financial partner. Normally, if there was any emergency, I would have heard from my purchasing partner who had long ago taken on the role of vice president of operations. Unfortunately, we had a little confusion about our vacation schedules, and this was the first time in our 12-year history that we were both off at the same time.

My financial partner, the CFO, was contacted by my executive assistant and office manager who was getting an earful from not one but three of my good representatives. Apparently, these reps were getting reports of compressed air flow meters and high flow natural gas flow meters reading incorrectly, and there was no doubt that something was seriously wrong. Since two of the owners were on vacation, she was the one taking these phone calls. She had no choice but to contact the CFO to discuss whether she should wait until I return or to phone me.

Well, he made the decision to call me himself. He reported that three of our best reps had reported calibration issues, all seemingly related to high flow applications. But this time, it wasn't related to the turbine issue, for that issue only dealt with low flows. One of my reps was fuming, according to him, because they worked very hard to secure this big account only to have the customer independently verify that the readings were off by as much as 15%. That is an enormous error; after all, our published specifications are close to 1%. I was in shock.

So, I phoned the rep who was most upset and learned that they were measuring compressed air at full capacity of their equipment, and the meter was reading 15% higher than the rated capacity of the compressor. Clearly, this was unacceptable. I then called the director of engineering and reported what I had heard from the rep and what, in addition, I had learned from our CFO. Since the reports all came in a cluster, I had hoped that it was some anomaly that had occurred and that it was not a pervasive problem.

When I returned four days later, I learned that there was a common denominator to the three issues: It was that we did not have a strong enough blower to take actual data at the higher flow rates, especially since all three applications were in large pipes

(4" or 6"). But in the past, that issue did not seem to be a problem since the data we did take generated a nice smooth consistent curve that could be extended mathematically (this extension is called "extrapolation"). And, to my knowledge, we did not have complaints prior to these recent reports.

However, since we could not fully simulate these high flow rates of these applications, we had no way to determine what was causing the issue. The solution was to get some help from one of the government facilities in Monterey. We had developed a relationship with some professors at this facility, and they seemed willing to do some testing for us.

We brought some meters in for testing, and our director of engineering drove to the facility to utilize one of their very high velocity and high flow standards to see if their results corresponded to our predicted calibration. The results were disturbing. The meters were all accurate where actual data was taken within the range of our blower, but the extended part of the curve was inconsistent. Sometimes the error was minimal, but depending on the choice of the method of extrapolating the curve (e.g., there were three different choices: a 3rd order, a 4th order or a 5th order, all different mathematical ways to linearize our data), the meter could read high or low. There seemed to be no rhyme or reason to the results.

We spent a few days analyzing the data, and yet we could not find any consistency, regardless of the math that we used. What was apparent was that the higher the flow rate specified, the worse the error might be. What we needed was a way to gather more data, so we could arrive at some approach that would eliminate the error. To do so meant going back to the government facility.

This time, we built up three meters, all set up for maximum flow. Armed with these additional meters, we decided to have them do a full air calibration on those meters over a full range, well in excess of the maximum flow rate that our facility could generate. Those meters read properly at the government facility, but when put in our facility, we still could not generate enough flow in the 4" pipes to simulate these high flow rates and velocities.

The solution was a bit novel and one which is a bit difficult to explain. The best way to explain it is to compare our facility to your household shower. Let's assume you turn the main valve on the shower to fully open. But if you have a sprayer fitting on the shower head, you have many choices as to how the water comes out. If you want a wide spray, you turn it to a wide spray position. But if you want the water to come out nice and strong, there is a different position on the fitting. What is really happening on the strong water position is that the fitting is restricted and the velocity increases. You can feel how fast the water is moving when the spray is concentrated as it comes out strong. There may be the same volume of water in both cases, but when the fitting is restricted, that volume is concentrated and the spray is narrow, yet it feels very strong. That "strong" feeling is the fact that the water is coming out much faster now.

In our facility, we had a choice of pipes (1", 2", 3", 4", etc.) all coming off of the same blower. Imagine if we had the blower at full capacity (just like the shower valve) and routed the air flow through the 4" facility. Doing so resulted in a slower velocity. If we switched to the 1" pipe, (still keeping the blower at full capacity) the velocity would increase greatly. Although there would be a little loss due to the pressure drop in the 1" pipe versus that of the much wider 4" pipe, we would be able to generate a much higher velocity of air through the 1" pipe versus the 4" pipe using the same blower.

Well, it turns out that a thermal mass flow meter, the type of technology that we manufacture, is based on the heat transfer at the point where the sensor is. And the sensor is always installed in the center of the pipe. So, the sensor in the above example would "see" a much higher velocity in the center of the 1" pipe versus the 4" pipe given the same volume coming off of the blower.

Or to put it more plainly, the higher the velocity experienced by the sensor in the center of the pipe, the more heat would be transferred by this fast-moving air (or gas). And the more heat transferred, the higher the flow reading. Specifically, the flow rate (which is what the customer is interested in), is based on the simplest of formulas: Flow equals Velocity times the pipe cross sectional Area (e.g., $Q = V \times A$). Yes "Q" refers to Flow in our industry.

So, let's go back to the problem we were trying to solve, using the example of a 4" pipe. In the 4" pipe, our blower was not producing enough velocity to simulate the highest readings that our compressor customers were trying to measure. So, if you are the inquisitive type, you might ask, "Well, why didn't you use a smaller pipe, such as the 1" pipe to simulate the customer's velocity, since its restricted cross-sectional area would have a larger velocity coming off of the same blower capacity based on the above formula?" That type of thinking is very astute. However, there was a problem, and it was due to geometry.

Our sensor is small, but it is not invisible. When it is put in a small pipe (such as a 1" pipe), it blocks part of the area of the pipe and it causes a blockage error. However, in a 4" pipe, that blockage is negligible. That is why we had been using a 4" pipe for a customer's with that size application (or for customers with larger pipes as well).

So, we had a conundrum. We needed to use a 4" pipe to generate good calibration data, but we were not able to get to a high enough velocity to simulate the high flow rate (high velocity) of the customer's application. However, in a 1" pipe, we would more closely simulate the customer's velocity that corresponded to their high flow rate. Unfortunately, the blockage error of the sensor (i.e., the shadow caused by the sensor in such a small pipe) caused the data to be inaccurate.

However, there was a solution. Since the government facility helped us by calibrating three of our flow meters with their powerful blower and large pipe calibration standard, we were able to temporarily use those same three meters to take data within our 1" pipe facility. And even though our 1" pipe had blockage, this time the blockage error in our facility could be corrected for since we had actual flow data of these meters from their facility.

This correction, called a transform function, allowed us to use the 1" pipe to generate an accurate high point in these challenging applications. This extra point eliminated the error that extrapolation was causing. This method went a long way to solve our problem by minimizing extrapolation for high velocity applications, but it was a temporary solution. We knew that ultimately we would need to upgrade our entire facility to be able to handle much higher flow (and velocity applications), and that discussion is in another chapter.

Okay, we solved our calibration uncertainty, but we had a long way to go to solve the loss of confidence that these three reps (and their customers) had in us. To make matters worse, these three in-cidences were not the only ones. As the weeks and months went by, more and more complaints started coming in from high velocity customers who had calibrations done prior to using the algorithm. I still had my hands full, and I was worried about our very existence.

Although we now had a solution to eliminate calibration er-rors, my biggest challenge was one of credibility. How do I re-assure these customers, and our reps that made the sale to them, that the problem has been solved? Sure, we would recalibrate their meters and return the corrected meters to them, but what about future orders. What about the reps trusting that this issue would not happen again?

Good reps don't just report a problem. Good reps visit the customer to try to resolve the problem first. They make extra visits and often act as intermediaries on behalf of their customers by trying first to resolve the issue with our service department, or in some cases, our engineering group. Under normal circum-stances, complaints are usually resolved in a timely manner. But with this issue, we were in the dark. It was not until we did the testing at the government facility that we understood what the problem was and fortunately learned how to solve it.

Meanwhile, until we had a solution, our reps were in the dark as well. And all of our reps do not just sell Sage. They sell many other products, such as valves, pumps, and a variety of other pro-ducts to satisfy their customers. Although by contract none of the products that they offer are competitive to our flow meters, not all of the products they sell are complementary to our flow meters. Some have nothing to do with gas flow and merely solve an unrelated need that their customer has.

The implication of having many products to sell is that they will focus on those products that not only offer the most value or best solution to their customers but those that are the most reliable. The last thing a rep wants to deal with is a problem. It is bad for their reputation and bad for their incomes.

All of us at Sage have worked very hard to build our business and to secure our reputation as a reliable, honest, and quality vendor. Furthermore, over the years, we have gone out of our way to offer extraordinary support to our reps, being responsive when they had questions, listening to them when they had suggestions, and providing them with a high quality and reliable flow meter.

This calibration issue, if it wasn't handled properly, could damage the hard-earned trust and relationship that we had developed with our reps. It also can discourage them from promoting our product, for fear that they will have after-sale issues that are costly and time consuming. Clearly, it was imperative that it be handled promptly and the ball was in my court to undo the damage.

Fortunately, I had always been truthful to my reps, and we had garnered good will by offering in-depth training and visits to assist them in promoting our product, and we always paid them their commissions promptly. Equally important was the strong relationships that I developed with many of the individuals selling our product.

So, my mission was to reassure each of my reps who had issues, or whose customers had issues, that the problem has been resolved, and I would further explain the unique circumstances that disguised the fact that we even had an issue until reports started coming in. In most cases, I was successful and my reps were willing to give us a second chance.

But the situation did take its toll, since it is one thing to re-assure a rep and it is another to reassure a customer. And in that regard, I volunteered to speak with their customers directly, although it was never easy. Customers seem to be inherently distrustful. I did my best to distinguish us from other situations and other companies that they may have encountered and offered my personal assurance as the president of Sage that the accuracy issues they experienced were an anomaly. I stressed that we have not only corrected the issue, but we have added numerous controls and systems to prevent a reoccurrence.

In closing, it took us many months to overcome the situation, especially since not all meters were promptly installed. Thus, just when we thought the last of the questionable calibrations were resolved, another customer would discover an issue from an older calibration, and we would have to deal with all of the unpleasant ramifications of an unhappy, and in some cases, bitter customer all over again.

Nevertheless, slowly but surely, we regained the trust and the mindshare of our reps. However, this painful period was not without its consequences: Our sales, which had been, on average, improving for 12 years, flattened out for the next two years. At least we weathered the storm.

CHAPTER 13

AN ABORTED RECOVERY

The first six months of 2016 started strong, and our sales level was picking up and so did our profit picture. Finally, in spite of the residue of the calibration issues, all seemed to be going in a positive direction. It gave us an opportunity to start the process of developing some new products to build upon our prior technical success. Our CTO was tasked with developing some concepts for new products and software that the marketplace was beginning to ask for.

And while he was putting his thinking cap on regarding new products and new technologies, our director of engineering was coming up with concepts to upgrade our calibration facility to directly handle the higher flow applications that were becoming more common. Our "work around" a few years earlier was getting us by, but we knew that we needed to put some serious dollars into investing in a much more sophisticated system. Especially with our renewed focus in the oil and gas industry (where high flows are required), we were committed to completing this upgrade project within 18 to 24 months.

We were feeling pretty good. Sales were up, shipments were up, and profits were up. And my staff was enjoying the challenges of keeping up with the demands of meeting our production lead times, as well as meeting specific customer delivery promises. Once again we could all taste success, and each of us felt that our many years of hard work and individual contributions over the years, as well as our joint efforts at growing a successful enterprise, were paying off.

For me personally, it was a time of reflection, realizing that we have built up something very important, where our customers were benefiting from our high-quality products, and behind the scenes, our workers were feeling the satisfaction of producing those products. Particularly satisfying was the fact that although our company was only a bit over 13-years-old, we had accomplished so much in that time period. We had started from scratch, literally from an empty building. But we had a lofty idea and a vision of improving the technology, providing the marketplace with a better thermal mass flow meter that did not drift over time, and a method to reassure customers that their meters were still performing accurately years after the purchase. Our early hopes were paying off.

In June of 2016, amongst the backdrop of two strong first quarters, the president of the Florida HVAC company contacted me. He wanted to set up a visit at my facility with not only himself but with his boss as well, who happened to be the VP of the parent company, the same company that in the past had been putting out signals to purchase us. This seemed like an exciting proposition, especially since we had such a strong relationship with the

Florida company and their business with us had grown substantially. We planned a dinner a few weeks in advance, and I looked forward to the meeting.

So, it was that at 5:05 PM, a few weeks later, after all of my staff had left, I saw the Florida president (presumably accompanied by his boss) approaching my office door. I welcomed them into my office and they sat opposite me at my desk. I asked them if they had smooth travels, and they acknowledged that the flight was on time and they had no issues.

But something about their body language didn't seem right. Their smiles were absent, and the warmth that I would normally see from the president was lacking. And then the president began to speak, and he said he had some news to share with me:

"We have come to tell you that we just closed escrow on an acquisition with your competitor, and we wanted to give you this news face-to-face."

"You're kidding?" I replied.

And then they went on to explain that since we did not show any genuine enthusiasm about being acquired by them, they had no choice but to pursue another well-respected Thermal Mass Flow manufacturer. Since such negotiations are confidential, there was no way to give me a heads up about their intentions until escrow closed. In other words, the sale is final. As such they wanted to communicate this critical news to me in person before an announcement would be made to the general public.

I am not sure how to express the shock that I felt when they dropped this bombshell. After all, for six years, we had a phenomenal working relationship with them, where everyone got along, where we delivered our products promptly, provided extraordinary service, and collaborated on improving our calibration and quality processes.

But what really hit me hard was the reality of losing our biggest customer, one who represented one fourth of our revenue and one third of our unit volume! In a nutshell, this news was devastating, and it meant that our very survival was now at stake.

As the vice president of the parent company took control of the conversation and expressed his empathy with our situation, his demeanor was actually apologetic. Perhaps that is why something deep within me kicked in. Rather than showing anger or expressing how catastrophic this news was to our business, words came out of my mouth that took no thought, almost as if it came from some place outside of myself.

I said, "Why don't you purchase both of us?" After all, aside from benefiting from the customer base and product offering of our competitor, you would also get the best of our technology and you would be stronger for acquiring both of us.

After a pause, the VP questioned if I was serious. I replied in the affirmative. And then after a second pause, this time a long one, he said, "You know, that may work out." And he continued, "The Chairman of the Board is in Switzerland right now, but I will text him to see what he thinks and I should know within a few days."

And then as they got up to leave, I said, "I guess I should cancel our dinner reservations." And the VP simply responded, "I will get back to you within a week."

So, I was left, sitting alone in my office, reflecting upon what had just happened, feeling that the bottom has fallen out of my world. Over 13 years of hard work and devotion in building up

Sage Metering, and this dream now seems to be crashing apart. I have no idea how to put it back together.

Worse yet, I have to share this devastating news with all of my partners and my most heavily invested partner, the CFO, is in Mexico on vacation. What will he think when I disclose this news upon his return?

My only solace was the hope that the VP of the parent company would have a positive response from his chairman. Short of that scenario, I had no idea how we could possibly survive a sudden drop in revenue of 25%.

CHAPTER 14

— —

MY PARTNER RETURNS

Three days later my partner, the CFO returned. I phoned him and reluctantly communicated the devastating news to him. I must have blocked out how he responded since I actually do not remember any of his comments. But I do know that we met the next day, at which point he presented a tentative proposal how to dramatically cut our expenses and overhead.

He said we need to take drastic measures, and we need to lay off at least six people, cut our own salaries, as well as that of the remaining employees. Furthermore, we need to be extremely careful with any discretionary expenses that can be delayed or perhaps eliminated completely.

The next day, I called an emergency meeting with all of our employees. I knew it would be difficult to share this painful news with them, but obviously I had no choice.

I started out the meeting reminding them that I have always been open and upfront, and I needed to share some very serious news with them. I then recounted what had happened on that fateful late afternoon when the visitors from the Florida company arrived, but I certainly made no mention of any prospect of us being acquired. However, I did underscore the severity of the situation and disclosed that we have no choice but to lay off five or six staff members. I said that after the meeting, we will disclose privately which staff members unfortunately need to be laid off. Then I went on to say that additionally, each remaining employee will have to take a temporary pay cut of 10%, although I explained that I honestly did not know how soon this hourly cutback would be restored. In addition, I shared that the four owners are each taking a 30% cut. And finally, I expressed that this action is our best chance of survival, but we have every intention to survive. And if all goes well, we may be able to rehire the laid off workers at some point in the future, assuming they are still available at that time.

After the meeting, we did in fact lay off five of our workers, who we felt we could temporarily do without, with the expectation that one of the remaining workers could take over his or her responsibilities. We also decided to terminate our international manager. I phoned him personally and described the onset and circumstances of the situation, and that in addition to us having taken the drastic measures described at the meeting, we also needed to do without an international manager. Essentially, I had to terminate his employment. Last but not least, I phoned our part-time marketing manager and I told him I needed to cut down his services to nearly no hours. I must say, both the international manager and marketing manager took the news as well as they could. Being professionals they understood that I really did not have a choice.

In retrospect, matters could have been a lot worse. All of the laid off employees were able to grasp the necessity of the action, and one of them in particular expressed her willingness to be re-hired at some future date, and if at all possible, she would rather wait to be rehired by us than to take a job somewhere else (in fact, 18 months later, we did hire her back). As for the employees who remained, as difficult as the news was, they appeared to under-stand. Not one of them chose to quit, and all of them continued to work just as hard as they had before the cutback. I could see that our culture of honest communication, genuine respect, and an environment that fostered inter-departmental collaboration seemed to have muted what could have been a much more emo-tional and painful experience, although in no way am I making light of the severity of the situation.

CHAPTER 15

———

THE DUE DILIGENCE PERIOD

The Florida company did in fact decide to pursue acquisition negotiations with us. However, I could see that being cornered, we had little leverage in discussing a sale price. Eventually, they proposed what turned out to be a very modest offer, but at least it was an offer. After a few days of meeting with my partners individually, as well as jointly, we decided that the risk of not accepting their offer was too great, even though there would be little money left over for our futures since our debt would first have to be paid off. But if we did not accept their offer, there was danger of not making a profit without them, even though we had cut our expenses to the bone.

So, after a thorough review by our attorney, we signed a Letter of Intent, agreeing to accept their offer, knowing that throughout the next four to five months, known as the due diligence period, we would determine if the offer would hold up. We fully understood that if during their financial and internal investigation they were to find any issues to be sufficiently disturbing, they could legally terminate the offer.

So, it was that over the next five months, we had to work especially hard to bring in as many sales as possible. After all, we still needed to cover our expenses, which were substantial in spite of the cutbacks on personnel and salaries. The challenge to do so was formidable since the loss of the Florida company's dependable monthly revenue could not easily be made up. We certainly advised all of our representatives that there were no longer any restrictions on selling to the commercial market, but going after a market that they hadn't been pursuing for the last six years is a very slow process.

Compounding the challenge to bring in more sales was the inordinate amount of paperwork and correspondence that was needed to respond to the questions associated with the due diligence process of the Florida company's acquisition questionnaire. It was nothing less than onerous. Hours and hours were spent retrieving historical data, as well as addressing a plethora of sales and marketing questions that took a great deal of thought to compile. This additional effort put a great strain on our ability to conduct business as usual, yet we had no choice.

So, we plodded along and finally completed the majority of their requirements. Yet, we also had to provide updated financial information as the weeks and months went on, and in addition, we had two separate visits from them for on-site inspections and more in-depth questioning.

And then there were the interviews with our owners, as well as some of our key employees and managers, although it was necessary to withhold disclosure of the purpose of these employee and manager meetings to keep the process confidential.

But by the end of the year, they had everything they needed for a final review and advised us that within a few weeks, they would confirm the escrow date at which time ownership of our company would pass on to them.

Any sale has tax consequences, and we had asked them to consider deliberately delaying escrow until early January, but we did not know if they would go along with that. As we waited for them to finalize the details of the closing, I received a phone call from the main acquisition manager. It was not what I expected. Their review process concluded that there were some issues in part related to the off-premises situation with our CTO, as well as to how our proprietary technology had been handled. They felt that this matter diluted their original assessment of our worth to them. They were willing to go along with an early January closing, but we would need to accept 12-1/2% less money than they had originally proposed. I told him I needed to discuss this with my partners and would get back to him.

That night I thought long and hard about this change in circumstance. The more I thought about it, the more incensed I became. Long before they contacted our major competitor, we had a meeting with them concerning acquisition since a new acquisition manager was introduced to us. We told him we would keep an open mind about acquisition but weren't quite ready. We left that meeting with the understanding that there would be ongoing discussions. But as the months passed, I never heard back from them. So, I began phoning them, but they never returned my calls. And then in June of this year, they blind-sided us with the news of just having acquired one of our main competitors. They never had the courtesy of giving us a heads up or at least contacting us to see if our position or receptivity to acquisition had changed. Furthermore, during the due-diligence process, my personal future was in doubt. They were putting all sorts of restrictions on me working with any competitors after a one year transition period of being held on as an employee. And finally, I had serious doubts that in the long run they would retain our facility, and in not doing so, it would cause great jeopardy to all my Sage employees. In a nut shell, this was a bad deal.

The following day, I called and said we decided not to accept their offer. He was shocked and said he would get back to me the next day to see if he could restore the offer back to its original value. Twenty-four hours later, he did call me and advised that their management agreed to retain the original offer. But it was too little, too late. My whole mindset had changed. I just didn't want to be associated with them in any way, nor did I now trust them. I simply said I am sorry, this no longer feels right. He was devastated; after all, they spent five months of reviewing and analyzing reams of data and they fully expected this deal to close, knowing full well that they had a bargain with us. But in the end, it no longer made sense to me. We would make it on our own without them!

CHAPTER 16

———

A DIFFICULT YEAR

We started the year off slowly, which is typically the case for the first quarter. Furthermore, without the regular commercial business, that quarter had a significant loss. We knew we had to reverse the trend, or we would run out of cash. One option was to find a competitor of the Florida company in the hopes of eventually making headway in that commercial market, even though we had relinquished that market for over six years.

That pursuit led us to a South Carolina company that made sophisticated air flow meters for the intake air in heating and air conditioning systems. This company had an excellent reputation in that slice of the market, and they had a strong national network of representatives who were calling on some of the same customers as the Florida company was calling on. Essentially, they were a commercial supplier in the HVAC (Heating, Ventilation, and Air conditioning) market as well. Coincidentally, during the time of our pursuit, they were also going through some rethinking of their own. They were well acquainted with the Florida company; after all, they were a direct competitor. But with the recent acquisition of a thermal mass flow meter company, the Florida company appeared to be even more of a threat than they were before. The South Carolina company began to feel vulnerable and they feared that they could lose their strong position in the marketplace for air flow meters to the Florida company if they did not come up with a more aggressive strategy.

Their approach to address this threat was to take on additional lines in the same industry by aligning themselves with quality suppliers who could provide the same products that the Florida company was providing. Their thinking was that they would need a full complement of HVAC products, so they, too, could address all of the product needs of large commercial contractors such as Siemens, Honeywell, and Johnson Controls, who tend to purchase from one source to meet all of their needs. If they had all of the relevant technologies in addition to their air flow meters, such as chilled water meters, steam meters, and of course, natural gas thermal mass flow meters that we produce, then they could begin bidding directly to the big contractors and their sub-contractors for commercial HVAC projects. They already had the national rep network and they felt that these reps could learn about new technologies and successfully promote them as well.

The first step of this new strategy was to create a separate marketing company consisting of all of these air flow representatives. That company would be a sister company to the air flow meter manufacturer and would pursue products in addition to their familiar air flow meters.

We contacted this company and began discussing the merits of our product. In short order, we had negotiated a contract permitting them to sell our natural gas flow meters at a substantial discount so they could compete with the Florida company. We designed flyers, assisted with training at their facility, and directly trained a few of their reps. Meanwhile, they also signed a contract with a Mid-Western company that supplied the other technologies. That company was very large but had little experience in selling into the HVAC marketplace. But by aligning themselves with the South Carolina marketing firm, they hoped to penetrate the commercial market with their help.

In some cases, the South Carolina firm set up joint trainings where we, along with the Mid-Western company, would educate the air flow reps about our respective technologies. We were all optimistic that this alliance would work out well and would generate new business for all of us.

As the months of 2017 rolled on, in spite of our optimism, little business developed from this new relationship. Sadly, the air flow reps, although skilled in promoting their product, were not making the transition to understanding how to promote the other technologies. Small orders did start coming in, but far less than anyone predicted. Nevertheless, it made no sense to dissolve the relationship, especially given the effort that had thus far been put in. The best approach was to keep training the reps, educating the prospects and promoting this joint effort, on the assumption that it will just take more time to develop.

Meanwhile, I could not stand idle. I decided to focus my energies on my own reps. By the summer, I was still not seeing the progress from our national sales manager in growing the domestic business, and I decided that I could handle it just as well without him. Although he had expertise on the marketing side, and over the last four years, he had helped direct our strategies to work more closely with the process industries, including oil and gas, I felt it was time to end the relationship. No doubt he had made a sales contribution, especially in hiring new representatives in areas that were weak, but his overall sales were flat and it no longer made sense to retain him. So, after officially terminating him (although I did provide him with a very positive letter of recommendation to assist his future employment), I took over.

As president I was already fully occupied running the business, so I had to gradually wean myself away from my executive responsibilities to make time for my sales promotional efforts. That transition took me the rest of the year to find a balance. Three months before the end of the year, I began planning for 2018. I started phoning my best representatives to set up future training trips with their sales staff that would allow me to make joint sales calls to their customers and prospects to promote our flow meters and our newly upgraded calibration facility (see next chapter). It took a while to lock in schedules, but I had succeeded in setting up six separate weeks with each representative through the end of April.

Of course, travel is not the only way to stimulate sales. While my very effective inside sales support manager was dealing with day-to-day quotes and orders, I was phoning the reps and assisting them with selling strategies. I also sent out monthly promotional newsletters to a few hundred of the salesmen and saleswomen domestically and to about 50 international distributors internationally. In addition, I directed my outside consulting staff to upgrade our website and I also periodically had conference calls with key customers while the rep was listening in.

Activity was picking up and the sales were beginning to grow. Contributing to this increase in revenue was the efforts of our fairly new Western Texas rep. They were gaining great traction with their oil and gas customers promoting our product for flare gas applications to meet environmental regulations. It turned out that even though they had only been with us for a little over three years, they ended up as our top representative. Unfortunately, in spite of our sales progress, it was too late in the year to make up for the deficit in the first quarter. As a result, we still suffered significant losses in 2017.

Fortunately, we had a good head of steam going into 2018 and we started off the year strong. My staff, seeing the more positive results after 18 tough months, appreciated my direct involvement. They knew that I was putting forth that extra effort to help grow the business, and it was reflected in their demeanor. They, too, began putting in that extra bit of energy and hard work, and the cumulative effect was one of a renewed sense of common hope that was pulsing through the company.

CHAPTER 17

UPGRADING OUR CALIBRATION FACILITY

In early 2016, management had proposed a more permanent solution to the high velocity applications that were becoming more common. This was not a simple "work around" that was established a few years earlier. This was a much more challenging project, and it was expected to take up to 18 to 24 months to complete and it would require substantial funding to implement it. It also involved the collaboration of much of our technical staff all working together towards the common goal of developing a very sophisticated automated calibration system complete with a 50 horsepower blower motor, extensive sweeps of new 8" stainless steel piping, the need for a heat exchanger that had to be mounted on a special platform near the ceiling, and the removal of a staircase that led to a second floor storage area (to be replaced with a foldable pull down attic ladder). We also would have to add an additional high amperage 220-volt electrical service and heavy duty wiring to run the blower. Furthermore, we would need to procure a very sophisticated positive displacement flow meter that would be retrofitted to the blower. Further still, the protective cabinetry for the blower, motor, and meter would be custom built and would require a crane to lift it out of a large transport vehicle and line it up with our delivery entry rollup door for the fork lift to retrieve it.

Over 100-man hours of programming time would be needed to generate the graphical interface and automation software that would run the entire system. Finally, the new system would have to be integrated into our low and medium velocity existing calibration facility, controlled by numerous high capacity electronic valves that open and close as required to route the gas flow though the appropriate pipes.

The decision to deploy such financial and personnel resources to this endeavor was a testament to our commitment to our customers to provide the most accurate calibrations for their needs. There had been anecdotal evidence that some of our competitors were "bending the rules," regarding their flow meter calibrations, by taking shortcuts that could result in errors that the customer was unaware of. However, we were committed to take the high road, even if it affected our reserve of cash and our bottom line.

Fast forwarding, the system was engineered and substantially completed within the 18 months. It took another three months of testing until we fully deployed the system. Officially, it went into full operation in October of 2017, and it could generate velocities as high as 400 miles per hour! Or in the parlance of a thermal mass flow meter, we could generate gas flows as high as 35,000 SFPM (which in an 8" pipe is equivalent to a gas flow rate of 12,000 standard cubic feet every minute!).

The implementation of our high velocity calibration system and the merging with our conventional blowers and other calibration systems has been a real success. It has allowed us to more effectively pursue the flare gas applications in the oil industry, as well as accurately measuring high flow rates of natural gas in the aluminum industry and other process applications. In addition, we could more effectively measure compressed air flow, a common application related to monitoring and controlling energy usage.

CHAPTER 18

———

A DRAG ON OUR TEAM

As you recall, the heroes who executed that ever so rare triple play were a cohesive group who worked hard over the entire season to hone their skills to near perfection. Most importantly was the respect and trust that each player held towards one another, and their willingness throughout the baseball season to recognize that their individual talents alone had little value, but their collaboration as a team was essential. Intuitively, they knew that a successful baseball season depended on a group effort, and this deep sense of interconnectedness was so strong that their instincts took over in executing the triple play; after all, at most they completed this remarkable feat in less than two seconds — there was no time for thought.

Sage Metering has espoused a similar culture from day one. However, as time went on, my partner, the CTO, seemed to be getting off track, and his behavior was clearly anathema to our unity. I thought I had successfully dealt with his confrontational behavior when I flew down to San Diego many years earlier to address his poor attitude. As the designer of all of our products, and the protector of our confidential source code, once again I had a challenge on my hands. At that time, I needed to articulate the fact that he was acting in a very unhealthy way for our company in that he was never taking responsibility for his actions and he was creating discord by criticizing others both verbally and in writing; and he became defensive whenever anyone, whether an employee, manager, or owner, tried to bring him evidence that there may have been flaws in his designs. To minimize his disruption to the company, I had reassigned him from engineering manager to CTO, a position that did not have any staff working under him. That responsibility was given to the newly appointed director of engineering.

Apparently, that transfer of responsibilities was not taken lightly since it appeared that he had little respect for the director, in spite of the fact that the director was an excellent manager, well-liked by all of the Monterey staff, and a very productive, loyal, and collaborative individual. Granting the director such sweeping responsibilities did not sit well with the CTO's viewpoint. Over time it festered within him, and towards the middle of 2017, it manifested in his nasty and disrespectful behavior towards the director (in his interactions and communications, as well as in his dismissal of any technical suggestions that the director had brought forth).

Once again I had to deal with this behavior and counseled him to show respect and to communicate in an open and professional manner. At first, it looked like I was getting through to him, but as the months went on, the situation deteriorated.

On at least three occasions, the CTO publicly showed disrespect to me in open meetings. Also, his productivity started dropping off. The new product development that he was responsible for was languishing, and not only was he way behind schedule in its expected timeline, but there were numerous times when we could not reach him by phone or even email. This was not normal. In the early years, he had always been available, productive, and hard working. Something had changed.

Worse yet, when we would review the status of the new product development, our test engineer would find flaws, but when he reported those observations back to the CTO, he denied that there were any design issues and blamed the test engineer on poor test methodology rather than trying to correct the issue.

His behavior was absolutely unacceptable and certainly was not healthy for our employees, or for that matter, for the company as a whole. And as an owner, his toxic behavior was even more unsettling for the staff. After all, the employees were obviously wondering why I was not doing anything about it.

Of course, I knew that his designs and product development were essential to our success and growth. I also knew that his repeated refusal to turn over a copy of our confidential source code to our main office was his way of holding us hostage.

By the middle of 2018, I felt that I had to take serious action, but I was torn as to how to reconcile his importance to our future continuity versus the cancer that seemed to be taking over the company due to his behavior. My gut told me that all my hard work in building up the company, creating a positive culture of job satisfaction, mutual respect, and collaboration were being jeopardized and could easily be undone.

But soon a series of other unforeseen situations occurred: Firstly, one of our long-term employees who had been handling all of the three-dimensional drawings and associated documentation, absolutely critical to our operations, gave notice that he had very serious family problems and would be leaving in two weeks. This was a major blow to us, especially to our director of engineering, who depended so heavily on his skill as a CAD operator. AutoCAD, sometimes called CAD or CADD, refers to computer-aided design or computer-aided design and drafting respectively. Finding a replacement for such a difficult skill, especially in a near full employment market, would be very difficult indeed. Secondly, and equally serious, was the sudden decision by our test engineer to leave for another company. He had become so frustrated with the reluctance of our CTO to take his test results seriously that he no longer wanted anything to do with him. And his skillset would also be very hard to replace. Finally, I could tell that our director of engineering was already at his wits end with the poor treatment and lack of co-operation he had been receiving from our CTO. I could see that he was getting more and more disenchanted with that situation, in addition to the sudden need to replace two critical staff members that he depended on. It occurred to me that the challenge to deal with all of these concurrent events might result in him looking elsewhere for employment — that would be the final blow to our company.

When the director called me into his office to speak with the test engineer who had just given notice (and in fact had already taken another job), I closed the door behind me and asked the test engineer what had transpired to cause him to make such an abrupt decision. He told me of his frustration and exasperation dealing with the CTO. He also was worried about the future of the company. I tried to appeal to him to stay, to reassign him to a situation that he would feel comfortable in. He was unwavering. He had made his decision. Not being able to persuade him to stay, in spite of my reassurances of the company's health, I simply could only wish him well.

But I wasn't done speaking. In the back of my mind was a greater urgency and the fear that if I did not act with courage at that moment, all would be lost. I had this nagging feeling that the director was the next to leave since he, too, has been pushed to the brink based on the absolute lack of cooperation and lack of respect exhibited by the CTO.

And suddenly the strangest thing happened. I looked directly at the test engineer and I said, "You know, if I wasn't the president of this company and a partner of the CTO but rather was hired as a consultant, what would I do? Knowing everything that had transpired, it would be unequivocal. I would recommend that the CTO be fired."

That is in fact what I did. I fired my partner.

As a responsible corporation with board members, it did take a process that followed over the next few days to convince my majority partner, the CFO, of the urgency of this decision. At first, he thought I was hysterical; after all, to him this decision seemed to come out of the blue. But I recently learned that an excellent design engineer was available who had worked closely with my director of engineering at another company many years prior. And I wanted to stress to him the critical nature of the timing in replacing the CTO.

I had two lengthy conversations with the chief financial officer that Friday afternoon, as well as over the weekend, but I was still having trouble getting through to him. I suggested that he meet privately with the director of engineering to get another perspective on my decision. That meeting occurred Monday, and after a while, I joined in as well. It took another 45 minutes, but the logic and necessity of my decision could no longer be questioned. Finally, we were all in agreement and it was just a matter of how to properly formalize the termination.

We had absolute justification for the decision, but nevertheless we counseled with our employment attorney to be sure we were following California law. We split up responsibilities: I would compose the termination letter and the CFO would prepare a severance pay document.

My termination letter was carefully written and basically focused on the facts, minimizing language that was overly personal or critical. Accompanying the termination letter was a severance document that offered severance pay (equivalent to six months of his salary) based on meeting certain monthly criteria. For example, the company's confidential source code was still in his possession, and we certainly did not want to send him any monthly funds until he returned our property to us.

Oddly, he refused to accept the conditions of the severance pay document, and thus we had no obligation to pay him. However, in light of his intransigence, it took a seven-month legal battle to secure our rightful proprietary source code, which essentially contained the "secret sauce" of our technological developments.

Shortly after he was terminated, we did hire the talented design engineer. We also had the good fortune of finding a skilled

CAD expert who happened to come out of retirement to respond to our online job description. Both new employees turned out to be highly skilled, motivated, and equally important, they naturally fit into our culture. These were professionals who sought a positive, yet challenging work environment, and as time went on, it became clear they were making a tremendous contribution to our growth.

As for the company as whole, terminating the CTO brought a breath of fresh air and renewed hope to all employees. In particular the engineering department was finally hitting on all cylinders. Everyone was getting along, collaborating, problem-solving, and enjoying the positive progress that finally was occurring.

Metaphorically, we were once again feeling that unity so similar to executing a Triple Play, but we also just had a literal Triple Play as well: 1, 2, 3: 1) We fired the disruptive CTO; 2) Hired a very talented replacement and; 3) Filled the CAD position with a very experienced computer draftsman – all achieved within weeks of each other. Yes, I was grateful.

CHAPTER 19

PROGRESS ON ALL FRONTS

With our new engineering employees, the development of our new flow meter product and our new software were now moving at a very rapid pace. And this progress was also due to much greater collaboration by all involved. Absent was the disruptive and destructive nature of our ex-CTO who had been restraining the development. Now there was a newfound freedom of expression, and ideas began flowing. The result was a much more innovative flow meter development than originally foreseen, in conjunction with an extremely user-friendly configuration and validation software program.

As there was technological progress on our soon to be introduced new products, my enthusiasm grew, and I imparted this new-found excitement to my reps and their customers as I began traveling around the country. We built up a preliminary demonstration flow meter that I would present during my trips, along with an early version of the software as well. We called the new thermal mass flow meter the Paramount™, and the new software was labeled SageCom™.

So, armed with the new flow meter and software, I went on the road and began conducting trainings, educating the reps on the uniqueness and differentiating features of these products. I would then make joint sales calls to their prospects and customers, and I would introduce our new products to them. The response from these sales calls was very encouraging. Everyone seemed to see the value of our improvements and appreciated the thoughtfulness and design elements that went into both the Paramount™ and the SageCom™. Clearly, this positive response heralded a bright new future for all of us.

It did take many months for the impact of my travels to take hold, but by the middle of the year, orders for the new product started coming in and our profitability began improving. Furthermore, new doors were opening due to the unique features of the Paramount™ and its accompanying software. Markets, such as the oil and gas industry, saw the benefits of being able to check the status (e.g., verify proper functionality) of our individual flow meters without interrupting the flow of the critical information coming from a network of Paramounts to their computers. In other words, this product had two independent communication channels, so they could easily connect our software to run validation routines to comply with quality control or environmental requirements without running the risk of losing data to their central computers from all of the other Paramounts on the same network. These features are analogous to a chain of Christmas lights, where if one light goes out, the rest may go dark, but with two channels, that cannot happen with the Paramount.

Complementing our sales efforts was an aggressive marketing campaign. The website was updated to feature the Paramount™, and it even included a 15-minute training video, which I developed covering the many features of the software. Additionally, new flyers and brochures were created and wiring diagrams were improved to simplify installation. To encourage our representatives to purchase demos, we offered a convenient carrying case, complete with all the likely accessories, power supply, the software, and of course, the new flow meter, priced affordably by offering a 50% discount.

And sure enough, orders from the reps started coming in for the promotional demo equipment, and thus they would be able to set up appointments on their own to promote the product to their customers. And as an added incentive, beyond the normal commission that is earned on any sale of our products, I added a special $100 bonus on this product to go to the individual sales person, not the rep firm, for each and every Paramount that they would sell at List Price.

In summary, our team, just like the baseball team that executed the triple play, was on a winning streak. And as the year went on, the business continued to grow.

CHAPTER 20

LOYALTY AND A POSITIVE CULTURE

We have all worked hard to get to this point in our growth, especially after overcoming so many challenges. Clearly, everyone in the company contributed to where we are today.

What has most impressed me about the staff is the trust they have had in our management in spite of so many setbacks. The employees have never lost faith in our ability to overcome adversity. They have hung on, even when the situation was bleakest. They have been loyal and committed throughout, and they have always taken pride in their work. Yet as a group, they have collaborated towards the company's success, as well as towards their own futures.

Having such a loyal and cohesive group of individuals would not have been possible without building a culture from the onset, which fully acknowledged the positive role that each employee has towards the group success. It is this recognition that we are all a part of the same playing field, each a contributor to greater whole. That is the foundation of a healthy company.

CHAPTER 21

———

EPILOGUE

As the founder of Sage Metering, I take pride in our accomplishments. But what brings me the most job satisfaction is seeing the emotional and financial growth of the employees over time. We have a disparate group, but each employee (with some guidance) has found his or her niche as to where they best fit in, and where they can make the most difference towards our company's growth, as well as to their own inner growth. By aligning their talents with their primary job function, they take that extra pride in their work and have the sort of job satisfaction so absent in corporate America. And through their uniqueness, they are the life force that drives our cumulative success.

This is where the analogy in executing the triple play is most obvious. The talented baseball players who executed the triple play each had their own personalities, egos, and strengths. But collaboratively, they achieved this very rare event, and as result, won the absolute prize: The World Series.

Very few businesses that start from scratch achieve success: According to the Bureau of Labor Statistics, 20% of small businesses fail in the first year, and by the second year, 30% fail. After five years, 50% fail. Finally, by year ten, 70% of small businesses fail. We are in year 17 and certainly have passed the statistical threshold of failure. It doesn't mean that we can let down our guard, but it does demonstrate that we are a rare breed, just as a baseball team that wins a world series is a rarity.

But rarer still is not just to survive but to thrive. And to do so takes the same ingredients that are common to our successful baseball team: Collaboration, trust, and respect, which I call "The Triple Play of Business." Sage Metering is a company that thrives. Our employees are content, feel purpose, and enjoy one another. They go home knowing they have made a difference, and they recognize that there is only a thin veil between management and their positions. Unlike so much of corporate America, where employees feel diminished, as if they are only "hired hands," at Sage we are all on the same page, regardless of one's position in the company; we all work together towards the greater good. This interconnectedness breeds success and is the essential element that has helped us overcome so many challenges in our growth.